School Ways

School Ways

The Planning and Design of America's Schools

Ben E. Graves

An *Architectural Record*/McGraw-Hill Professional Book Group
Co-publication

Edited by Clifford A. Pearson

McGraw-Hill, Inc.

New York St. Louis San Francisco Auckland Bogotá Caracas Lisbon London Madrid Mexico
Milan Montreal New Delhi Paris San Juan São Paulo Singapore Sydney Tokyo Toronto

Library of Congress Cataloging-in-Publication Data

Graves, Ben E.
    School ways : the planning and design of America's schools / Ben
E. Graves ; edited by Clifford A. Pearson.
        p.   cm.
    "An Architectural record/McGraw-Hill professional book group
copublication."
    Includes index.
    ISBN 0-07-002468-5
    1. School buildings—United States—Design and construction—
History.   2. School buildings—United States—Planning—History.
I. Pearson, Clifford A.   II. Title.
LB3218.A1G73   1993
727'.0973—dc20   92-29550
                                                  CIP

1 2 3 4 5 6 7 8 9 0   HAL/HAL   9 8 7 6 5 4 3 2

ISBN 0-07-002468-5

*The sponsoring editor for this book was Joel E. Stein, the editing supervisor was
Caroline Levine, and the production supervisor was Suzanne W. Babeuf. It was
set in New Century Schoolbook and Futura by North Market Street Graphics.*

Book format design: Marc Zaref Design, New York

Printed and bound by Halliday Lithographers.

To Larry Perkins who introduced me to the exciting world of educational facility planning and to Harold Gores who taught me to not be afraid to question the past.

School Ways has been made possible, in part, by the generous sponsorship of Brick Institute of America.

Long dedicated to educational issues, Brick Institute of America is playing an active role in building America's schools. As any tour of old and new schools will show, the association of brick and educational facilities has been firmly established for many years. Without a doubt, brick will continue to play an important role in the design and construction of tomorrow's schools.

Brick Institute of America.
11490 Commerce Park Drive, Reston, Virginia. (703) 620-0010

Contents

Acknowledgments

Anyone who has attempted to write a book quickly learns that it is not a one-person effort. Thankful appreciation is expressed to the many architects who responded to my request for information about their projects—past, present, and future. A special thanks to the members of the AIA Committee on Architecture for Education who advised me and shared stories of their successes and failures. I use as a resource and often quote from many of the books and studies from Educational Facilities Laboratories (EFL). It was my good fortune to be part of the staff of this organization and eventually to head it. To all the staff members who remember the original offices at 477 Madison Avenue with fondness, thanks for leaving me with the valuable source of reference material. I must mention Jonathan King, Alan Green (who left us too soon), Ruth Weinstock, and, of course, Harold Gores, who was our leader and inspiration.

EFL entered the scene in 1958. Founded by the Ford Foundation to encourage and guide constructive changes in school and college facilities, EFL based its programs on two principles:

1. Facilities should be more sensitively designed to the new needs of education in a period of rapid, indeed revolutionary, change in instruction and social conditions.

2. Economy is critical in an inflationary period, so intelligent economy should be encouraged wherever, whenever, and however it can be.

That is not too bad a charge for planners today. Our "education President" is encouraging interest groups to ask for a "new EFL." My advice is to proceed with caution. EFL was successful because it was independent and not tied to any interest group. We had only to answer to our board, who made certain we made grants that produced results that were truly experimental, would advance the knowledge of facilities planning and building, would be applicable to other institutions facing the same perplexing conditions, and would have sufficient leverage to bring brains and money to work, solving the facilities questions besetting schools and colleges.

I entered the EFL arena in 1965 after six years with Perkins & Will Architects. My first assignment was to head a study on how to upgrade our older school facilities. I dubbed the study "New Life for Old Schools." Later I opened an office for EFL in Chicago. After a brief period with two other architectural firms, I returned to EFL and opened an office in Austin, Texas. By this time, 1971, EFL had become a self-supporting organization with the staff serving as consultants to a wide variety of clients. In 1979 EFL became a division of the Academy for Educational Development. I formed my own organization, Educational Planning Consultants, in 1988. The request for the early EFL publications continues to this day. There is a need for such an organization. My hope is that if we reinvent the wheel, it will still be round.

A big nod of appreciation must go to Stephen Kliment and Clifford Pearson of *Architectural Record* who asked me to do this book. Along with Joel Stein of McGraw-Hill's Professional Books Group and Susan E. Davis, they gave me the needed direction and guidance along the way.

Not to be forgotten is Karen Lesmez who never complained as I made change after change, which she recorded in her trusty word processor. And thanks to my wife, Jane, who never complained when my nights and weekends were taken with the book's preparation.

To those architects whose work is not included, it was not because of quality. Space limitations were the usual reason. There are exciting things going on in the world of school planning. Even faced with all the detractors who find fault with the American education system, there are still those dedicated architects, educators, and school boards planning inspired educational environments for our children.

Keep up the good work.

Ben E. Graves

School Ways

Emerging Trends in School Design

C. William Brubaker

Audio-visual equipment such as film projectors (opposite) were once at the cutting edge of educational technology. Today computers (above) are the latest tools.

Having been involved in school architecture for many years, this author has seen the pendulum swing back and forth—from individual classroom cells to the open plan, from national priority to national disgrace. Certainly such swings of fortune and changes in attitude are not limited to the planning and design of educational buildings. We are a nation of great resources but limited attention spans. When we set our minds to a task, we usually do it well. After proving that we can do something well, we often stop doing it. Eventually, a crisis develops and we rediscover the importance of whatever we stopped doing.

After defeating dictatorships in Europe and Asia in the 1940s, America went about performing the more pleasant tasks of peace. We built families, and houses, and lots of schools in the 1950s and early 1960s. When the so-called baby boomers came of age, though, we stopped thinking of schools. By the late 1980s, we began to realize how neglect and changing demographics had created enormous problems with our educational system. In some parts of the country, schools were falling down or terribly outdated, while in other parts they were in short supply. By the early 1990s, schools were once again a buzzword on the tips of millions of tongues.

Being an optimist, this author would like to think we have learned from our previous mistakes and also believes that certain changes in philosophy and advances in technology represent permanent improvements in our educational system, and not just cyclical adjustments to current conditions. Some of the emerging trends that will shape future schools in the United States are discussed in this Introduction. Without exception, these trends represent important advances in the way we plan and design schools. It is this author's belief that our children and grandchildren will be taught in schools that will be the best ever.

Schools Will Be Held in High Esteem. Why? Because lifelong learning will be considered important to more people. School design, which had been neglected when enrollments declined in the late 1960s and 1970s, will again be a hot topic, as fresh demand for new facilities raises awareness. More citizens will recognize that architecture for education can make a difference in the quality of learning they and their children can enjoy.

Schools will be regarded as community centers serving all the people—places where everyone wants to be for education, culture, and recreation. Schools will be recognized as important institutions and will be planned as part of the broader community. They will respond to and affect neighboring buildings and open spaces. No longer will an educational facility stand alone, fenced off from neighbors, serving just a few grades of students on a rigid schedule, five days a week, nine months a year. Tomorrow's school will serve as a continuing education center for all those people within walking distance or a short drive, people of all ages.

The school is often the largest and most important building in a neighborhood. As a result, its planning and design are particularly important. In the "education age," expect educational facilities to attract the best talent in planning and design, and earn important design awards.

Winnetka, Illinois, serves as a fine example of people in a community recognizing the importance of their school system and the value of good architecture. Two generations ago, the superintendent of schools, Carleton Washburne, and the Winnetka Board of Education selected Eliel Saarinen and Perkins & Will to design a new elementary school to serve an evolving educational program. Completed in 1940, Crow Island School is now seen by many experts as the first modern school building. By designing a building that responds to an innovative educational program, that works on a child's scale and establishes a close relationship between indoors and outdoors, the architects pioneered a new direction. In 1990, Winnetka residents celebrated the school's 50th birthday with a year-long party emphasizing the importance of educators, architects, and the community working together.

We Will Reconsider Some Basic Assumptions. The size of schools is a good place to begin. Most people believe that a high school of 2000 students is a better place to learn than one with 3000. And both are better than one with 4000 students. Let's face it: Some large schools just grew without master plans.

Now there is new interest in smaller schools. Because of their more modest size, these facilities are seen as being more agreeable in scale, less threatening, and less institutional. It is also easier to acquire adequate real estate for them. In the long run, these institutions prove to be much more flexible. Three smaller high schools, for example, are more adaptable to changing conditions and enrollments than is one large school.

New technology—including television and computers—may also help make small schools more effective. By linking schools electronically, such technology may eliminate the need to have certain facilities and resources in every school. If a student can take an honors math class or gain access to specialized physics books by computer, for example, then a lot of duplication of facilities can be eliminated. Not every school will have an honors math classroom, although every one will offer the course. This might mean a return to 200-pupil elementary schools, 400-pupil middle schools, and 800-pupil high schools. With electronic assistance, smaller schools may become increasingly appealing.

Smaller schools may very well combine with other developments such as office buildings or even shopping malls to create a new kind of school system—one that is multilocational in nature and dispersed throughout the community. Utilizing many community resources, such a system would be highly flexible and able to offer students a broad range of choices for learning. Essentially, the school system becomes one great "network school" composed of a variety of small schools linked electronically and by buses or vans. In such a system, the computer and television are used as basic resources, just as books and periodicals are used today. The network includes community resources such as the local art center, museum, city hall, health center, community college, offices, laboratories, and factories. Each student progresses at his or her own rate with a specially designed curriculum. The student's schedule varies from day to day, as does the actual place of learning. The student may go to city hall for a government class, or the museum for history, or the performing-arts center for drama. Individual study, small-group discussions, and conferences with teachers occur at the student's home school where each student is allotted space for individual study. Back in 1977 this author and coworkers referred to individual study space as "turf."[1]

School Hours Will Be Reevaluated. Expect longer schooldays. Learning will not be limited to 8 a.m. to 3 p.m. Schools will be open earlier in the day and later in the evening to serve adults as well as children. Expect schools to be open seven days a week and 12 months a year. Flexibility will be a key to learning schedules in the future. Some students may use the school during the evening hours, while others may find Saturday a good day to learn. Some students may go to school March through December, but not in January and February. Architecturally, little has to change. (Durable materials and proper orientation to both summer and winter sun should solve most of the problems generated by extended schedules.) Economically, the all-day, all-year (year-round) school makes great sense since such a facility will be used more efficiently. By extending hours and access, a school can accommodate a greater number of people, reducing the need to open new schools or expand existing ones.

The Grade System Will Change. Long criticized as being too rigid and arbitrary, the existing grade system will finally yield to a system of "continuous progress," in which students will advance at their own rate. Students will work according to their curriculum tailor-made to satisfy their personal needs and goals. (While specialized curricula may not be used in the lower grades, they will certainly be tried in high school.) The old pattern of identical groups of 30 students sitting in identical classroom cells for standard 50-minute periods—the "cells and bells" system—seems to be doomed. Individualized programs are the wave of the future, and computers will help make them manageable.

The Needs of Teachers Will Be Considered. To make better use of the highly educated, well-paid teachers of the future, architects will be asked to design better workplaces for them. Every teacher will have his or her own work area, properly equipped with telephone, computer, and space for planning, preparation, and counseling.

Greater Choice Will Be Available. Students and parents will have more choices in the types of schools and kinds of educational programs available to them. The comprehensive high school will survive, but a broad variety of other options will also be offered. For example, magnet schools, offering specialized programs in science or the arts, will be home base for some students and part-time resources for others. Education will be a multi-locational experience.

Vocational-technical schools will undergo similar kinds of changes. More options, targeted more specifically on careers, will be made available. Students will attend classes at school, and then spend time at a health-care facility or a day-care center, for example. For some students, part of their education will occur at home.

Some schools will be designed and built for specific groups of students with special needs, such as those with severe emotional or physical handicaps. An excellent example is P.S. (Public School) 233 in New York City, which was created to serve physically handicapped students (p. 143).

Responding to all these changes, architecture for education will become more varied—sometimes dynamic and changing, sometimes stable and serene, often mixed with other kinds of development. In the future, an elementary school may be in the same building as a shopping center; parents will pick up their kids and the groceries on the same car trip. A high school may be in an office building; students will learn accounting in a real office.

While suburban and rural schools will continue to be buffered by open space, urban schools will feel increased pressure to fit into increasingly dense contexts. Architects will be asked to make these city schools respond to their surroundings and fit into their communities. As land values exert greater pressures, city schools may have to look up for space; 5 to 12 stories may be necessary to house these facilities. Elevators will become important features in these schools. A few existing schools, such as the 9-story Roberto Clemente High School in Chicago and the new Stuyvesant High School in New York City (p. 152), depend heavily on escalators. In some cities schools will be found in high-rise buildings, whether residential or commercial. Other urban schools may sit on two or more blocks, bisected by streets. In some cases the school will physically bridge the streets. The Whitney Young Magnet School in Chicago, for example, bridges West Jackson Boulevard.

Technology Will Change Education. New teaching and learning technologies—such as computers, video-display terminals, electronic notebooks, telephones, and fax (facsimile) machines—are already changing the way children learn. They will continue to evolve.

For example, in 1991 Sony introduced its Data Discman, a portable, palm-sized electronic book player, which provides on one disk access to *Compton's Concise Encyclopedia* and other resource books. One disk holds up to 100,000 pages. In other words, a student can carry a small library in one hand. Some of this new technology will require special wiring and furniture, and school architecture will have to accommodate it. Architects will have to remember, however, that computers and video-display terminals are tools, not ends within themselves. They are new kinds of "books" that will require proper "shelves." But just as bookshelves do not make a library, computers and video equipment will not make a school.

The proliferation of such technology, however, raises some interesting questions. Will students continue to "go to school"? Or will they work at their computers at home? The same kinds of questions are also being asked in the business world. Will people go to the office or work at home? To some extent, more people will, indeed, do at least some work at home. But there are limits to the effectiveness of machines. And just as there are advantages to face-to-face communication in business, there are important educational reasons to maintain the many human encounters—both planned and spontaneous—that can happen only in a formal school setting.

Energy Conservation Will Once Again Influence School Design.

Energy conservation, windows, and compact floor plans are interrelated issues that school architects will have to address. In the 1960s, when oil was cheap, air conditioning became common in schools. After the Arab oil embargo of 1973, the cost of energy skyrocketed and architecture responded, although not always in the best way. For example, some architects designed schools in which all functions were pulled into one large building, minimizing rooms adjacent to outdoor spaces and thus reducing the loss of heat during the winter and air conditioning in warm months. Such schools with large unrelieved footprints, however, meant that many classrooms were windowless. In fact, at one point the Florida legislature passed a law requiring all schools to be air-conditioned and windowless—an approach that understandably proved to be unpopular with anyone who had to spend more than half an hour in such buildings. Within a few years, a backlash had set in and the legislature passed a new law requiring operable windows for all classrooms. The quality of school design improved overnight! Not only were the new schools more enjoyable places in which to work and learn, but because the Florida climate is agreeable for most school months, the buildings proved to be energy-efficient. By taking advantage of cross-ventilation, the schools showed that energy conservation doesn't always involve complicated equipment and expensive machinery.

As it turns out, architecture thoughtfully attuned to nature holds the promise of better learning environments at the lowest costs. The key is to design buildings that respond to local climates and to learn from older buildings. It's time to reconsider, for example, the old California, Texas, and Florida "finger plan" campuses, which when properly oriented and shaded, provide classrooms with both natural light and natural ventilation. At their best, these school campuses offer agreeable gardens and comfortable settings for learning. When energy prices rise once again, perhaps then we will reexamine these facilities to see what lessons we can learn from them.

Flexibility Will Continue to Influence School Planning and Design.

Although schools are hardly businesses of learning, there are some interesting parallels between school design and office-building construction. The modern office building, for example, is a splendid example of adaptable space. When a speculative building is planned, the developer does not know who the tenants will be or even how many tenants there will be. As a result, the developer provides flexible space that can be subdivided to satisfy the particular needs of each tenant.

This is an important lesson for school planners. Curricula will change. Technology will change. Class sizes will change. Educational approaches will change. And school buildings should be able to accommodate these changes comfortably. A good school is never "finished." It evolves and adapts as people and programs evolve.

In addition to facilitating internal changes, most schools need to anticipate both growth and contraction. Past performance has not always been satisfactory. Too few schools are designed with future expansion in mind. But every school needs a master plan to accommodate changes in program and increases in enrollment. The opposite situation is also often ignored. What can be done when enrollment declines? The most common responses are to (1) recycle part or all of a school building for new purposes (housing, offices, or community center) as dictated by need and location and (2) reduce the size of the school by hauling away relocatable classroom units (an approach mandated in California).

Providing flexibility is a particular challenge for the architect. Three decades ago, one response was to create big, open spaces—uncommitted (and often anonymous) spaces. Sometimes it worked well, but usually the spaces remained dull and characterless. Associated with the open-plan approach to school design, these large, flexible spaces were intended to encourage larger groups of students and teachers to meet and work together. As often as not, the teachers never supported the approach, preferring their own classrooms in which they could close the door. During the 1970s and 1980s, most open-plan spaces were subdivided with new soundproof walls to create more traditional 800-square-foot classrooms. Some of these rooms, though, were windowless, creating a different problem for the unfortunate students and teachers.

With flexibility once again a buzzword, educators are hoping to learn from past mistakes. Instead of designing ill-defined spaces, school architects are devising systems of movable partitions that allow teachers to create a variety of different spaces. Attention is also being paid to flexibility in mechanical and electrical systems, so that walls can move without requiring changes in ductwork or piping. The same is true for computer and new communications systems; movable-partition systems must provide cabling so that terminals can be plugged in wherever they are needed. Currently, such systems usually rely on copper wire or fiber optics located in conduits in walls and floor slabs or in cable trays in ceilings. If wireless systems emerge, architects will have to respond.

School facilities represent a range of investments, each with its own life expectancy. The structural shell of a school building is a truly long-term investment, lasting 100 to 200 years. Mechanical and electrical systems, on the other hand, tend to wear out in 30 years. Room partitions, furniture, and other equipment may change every few years. Some electronic equipment may prove to be obsolete in a year or two. When planning for future contingencies and future needs, architects should keep these investment periods in mind.

Schools Will Be Imbued with Their Own Special Spirit. While office buildings may teach school architects a few lessons on flexible space, schools are quite different in terms of program and character. A speculative office building has no specific users, and the particular needs of its future tenants are unknown. In contrast, a school is designed for a particular educational program specifying the number and size of classrooms, laboratories, and common facilities. Just as importantly, every school—like every human being—should have its own special spirit. Although unquantifiable and often difficult to describe, this personality is a reflection of the school's educational approach, teachers, administrators, and students. The best school architecture somehow captures the essence of an institution's character—picking up in its materials, common spaces, siting, relationship with the outdoors, or basic organization the elements that make the school distinctive. Whether it is a courtyard perfect for informal gatherings or the quality of light that strikes classrooms or the innovative use of brick courses, special features that go beyond the basic outlines of a program can imbue a school with an invaluable asset: character.

Certainly the 800-square-foot classroom will continue to dominate educational programs, although a few team-teaching programs are once again calling for semiopen spaces. While architects will have to handle the standard classroom, they must be aware of a danger: Uninteresting rows of boxy spaces lining long corridors can crush a school's spirit. Good architects search for new kinds of spaces and special spatial events to relieve the predictable character of classrooms. We need the occasional idiosyncratic detail or surprising space to bring school architecture to life. While the straightforward and rational structural grid will usually prevail, opportunities for spatial variety should not be missed.

Overly energetic attempts to achieve high efficiency in net-to-gross areas can deaden a school. Educators and architects must resist such a mindset and should allow for the incidental unprogrammed spaces that can enhance the learning environment—activity nodes in the circulation system, informal gathering places, galleries, commons, and courtyards.

Community Schools Will Become Increasingly Common. Interest in lifelong learning and growing needs for cultural and social centers will add impetus to the existing community school movement. In the past, schools were for children and facilities were locked up at the end of the schoolday. Today, entire communities see the school as a vital resource for adult education, year-round recreation, and cultural activities. As a result, school buildings are open day and night, on weekends, and in the summer. Now everyone in the community goes to school to read in the library, attend theater performances, play basketball in the gym, attend public meetings, and find childcare services. The community high school consists of three major groups of facilities: (1) the learning center, including classrooms, laboratories, library, and media center; (2) the cultural center, including theater, shops, and music and art studios; and (3) the fitness center, including gyms, swimming pools, tennis courts, and locker rooms for both students and adults.

Since more people will be involved in schools—even those adults without children—there will be greater support for educational programs. More people will be involved in planning schools, coordinating open-space systems and building masses, and making these facilities integral parts of the larger community. As a result, school planning will be considered as one part of the larger process of planning community facilities, neighborhood shopping, and local parks. The interaction between school and locality will work both ways. Not only will more adults go to school for recreation and culture, but more students will visit city halls, local businesses, and other regional resources.

The planning and design implications of these new attitudes are clear. The school will no longer be a walled and isolated fortress, but will become an integrated part of the community as a whole. Since all generations will share educational facilities, schools will be designed with both students and adults in mind. A shop or studio, for example, will need storage for both student and adult projects. Separate locker rooms may be needed for recreational areas. The library will have messenger and electronic links to other informational centers. And since buildings will be used at night, the lighting of entrances, walks, drives, and parking lots will take on new importance.

Not surprisingly, tomorrow's comprehensive high school will be bigger. With more people using the institution and more activities taking place there, the school will have to grow physically. Demands for equal athletic facilities for women will also require more land and larger buildings. Growing sensitivity to environmental concerns will also result in more land being set aside for wetland and woodland protection. There is no question that sites will get bigger.

Because they will increasingly be community facilities, schools will be planned as part of local park systems. In Irvine, California, for example, schools are built in conjunction with parks—swimming pools and tennis courts are usually in the park, while baseball and soccer fields are usually on the school site. But with no fences separating the facilities, it is hard to tell where the school starts and the park ends. Pedestrian paths and bicycle trails connect the various facilities, minimizing contact between cars and pedestrians. At Ft. Collins High School in Colorado, Perkins & Will tied the school not only to local parks and residential areas, but to the neighborhood shopping center. So after dropping off your child, you can pick up the groceries or buy a new computer printer. By reducing the number of car trips, such planning reduces traffic congestion and air pollution, while making people's lives a little easier.

Renewal of Existing Schools Will Be a High Priority. Even if we wished to do so, it will not be possible to replace all old schools with new ones. Each older building must be evaluated separately to determine whether it can be successfully renovated at reasonable cost. In addition to a school's physical condition, its historical significance and place in a community's social fabric should be considered when deciding its fate. Although restoration of old buildings is labor-intensive work, many old schools built in the first three decades of this century are still structurally sound, firesafe, and architecturally distinctive. A good percentage of these buildings offer enough adaptable space to accommodate new programs and equipment.

Mixing old and new buildings on one campus is another approach that will probably be used increasingly in the future. Such a mix not only brings a sense of visual and historical diversity to a school but also allows renovation to progress in stages and ensures that all buildings will not become obsolete at the same time in the future.

In January 1992 the Association of School Business Officials (ASBO) released a study showing that 12 percent of all school buildings in the United States are inadequate. Tens of thousands of schools are currently in need of renovation or replacement, representing a major challenge for governments and architects in the 1990s.

Regionalism Will Flourish. Different climates, geography, economics, politics, building materials, cultures, and design traditions generate different architecture for every community. Just as fingerprints vary for every individual, so should design vary for each school project. New England's compact red-brick buildings are (appropriately) quite unlike the Pacific Northwest's wood structures or Florida's stucco buildings. Multistory urban schools, standing close to neighbors and strongly influenced by them, are in sharp contrast to single-floor suburban schools in park settings. Southern Californian architecture gives a Los Angeles school a special character, but would be totally inappropriate for a Minneapolis building.

When this author's firm, Perkins & Will, designed Capital High School in Santa Fe (pp. 95–97), the associate architect, Kass Germanas of Mimbres Inc. in New Mexico, spent days with us exploring on foot the architecture of old Santa Fe: the building forms, spaces, materials, colors, and traditions. Those experiences and images influenced the design of the school. As a result, the school draws inspiration from the area's long-established Territorial style of architecture and responds to the particular demands of the local climate. This attitude is in sharp contrast to the all-too-frequent practice of designing virtually the same building throughout the country. The same vaguely Postmodern entrances, the same basic massing, the same fenestration occur on schools from coast to coast.

For the same reasons that uniform designs are inappropriate, national standards for area per student and cost per square foot make no sense. In California, a skilled architect can design a good high school with a space budget of only 90 square feet per student, while in the Midwest, a quality secondary school may require twice that figure. Why the difference? Because in California the campus plan works. By placing circulation and some dining, assembly, and physical education facilities outdoors, the campus plan reduces the amount of indoor space necessary. Obviously, regional differences are powerful design generators.

As education is changing, so, too, is architecture for education. Diversity is now the norm—whether it is in educational programs and approaches or architectural responses. The American people are a diverse lot, coming from strikingly different ethnic and cultural backgrounds, demanding different services from their local school boards and holding varying aspirations for themselves and their children. Culture, climate, geography, and traditions differ greatly from town to town and state to state. The best school design celebrates these differences.

Note

1. Stanton Leggett, C. William Brubaker, Aaron Cohodes, and Arthur Shapiro, *Planning Flexible Learning Places,* McGraw-Hill, New York, 1977.

1

The Continuing Need for New Schools

School construction is influenced by three primary forces. The leading one is enrollment. If the number of students increases because of population growth or in-migration from other parts of the country, new construction is often the most appropriate way to accommodate additional students. A second factor is program. Program requirements today go far beyond the typical classroom and include accommodating facilities for such special groups as very young children, foreign students learning English as a second language, and gifted and talented students, to name just a few. The third influence is the need to replace or remodel outmoded existing facilities. As buildings and equipment deteriorate because of age or inadequate maintenance, this factor has become an increasingly important one. The Education Writers Association has estimated that one-quarter of all U.S. public schools need basic maintenance or major repairs. In Chicago alone, two-thirds of the city's 601 public schools are estimated to be in critical need of repair. The price tag to repair and replace the city's aging schools and ease severe overcrowding is estimated at $1.075 billion. Los Angeles reports a $1 billion need, and a study conducted by this author reveals that New York City has $17 billion in total school-building needs. The problem, however, is not limited to large cities, but is nationwide.

Judging from current demographics and enrollment figures, school construction and renovation will be necessary to meet increased demand for as far into the future as we can currently project. How that construction can best meet changing program requirements makes long-term planning absolutely essential.

What the Numbers Indicate

To try to predict the future, it is necessary to borrow crystal balls from various sources. At the beginning of the 1990s, most sources agree that the school population and the population as a whole is growing but at a slower pace than in the past decade. At the same time, the 65-year-old-and-older population is growing—and will continue to grow—faster than the population as a whole. Minority groups are the fastest growing segments of all. Since the second half of the 1980s, the nation's birth rate has picked up, as aging baby boomers finally decided to start having families and younger couples decided not to wait.

The total 5- to 17-year-old school-age population, according to most sources, is on the threshold of a relatively brief period of expansion. According to a report from the Educational Research Service, an analysis of the latest Census Bureau statistics concludes that the estimated 45,630,000 school-age children in 1990 are projected to increase in number to a high of 49,011,000 in 1998, a 7.4 percent increase. The total school-age population will then experience an extended period of decline which will not bottom out until 2015, when it is projected to hit 45,251,000, or 7.7 percent fewer than in 1998 (Fig. 1.1). Estimates of school populations by age groups show the greatest increases for younger students (5- to 9-year-olds) during the first half of the 1990s, followed by increases in the number of older students (10- to 17-year-olds) during the second half of the decade and beyond (Fig. 1.2). Defining the projection by ethnic group, it is estimated that between 1990 and 2010, the school-age population of blacks, Hispanics, and other races will continue to grow faster than that of whites.

Figure 1.1 **Estimates and Projections of the Total School-Age Population of the United States for Selected Years: 1980–2025.**

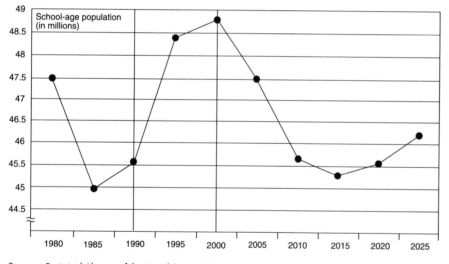

Sources: *Statistical Abstract of the United States 1981*, 28; *Statistical Abstract of the United States 1986*, 28; and U.S. Bureau of the Census, *Current Population Reports*, Series P-25, No. 1018, 42–87. (Reprinted by permission of Educational Research Service from *Demographic Influence on American Education, 1990*, Arlington, Virginia.)

The school planner has to look at all areas of the population. For instance, when funding is sought for school construction projects, a majority of retired voters can have an obvious impact on the outcome of any school-bond issue. Senior citizens may not be as willing as young parents to fund new school construction. This will be especially true as the 65-year-old-and-older population steadily increases. The Census Bureau estimates that by 2025 there will be 46.2 million school-age children and 59.7 million persons at least 65 years old, or 1.29 senior citizens for every school-age person (Fig. 1.3).

Figure 1.2 **Estimates and Projections of the School-Age Population of the United States, by Age Groups, for Selected Years: 1980–2025.**

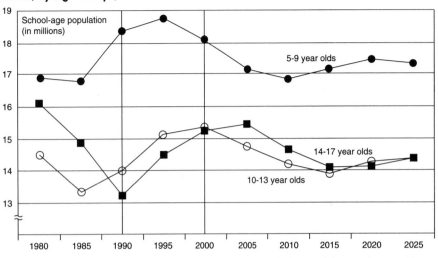

Sources: *Statistical Abstract of the United States 1981*, 28; *Statistical Abstract of the United States 1986*, 28; and U.S. Bureau of the Census, *Current Population Reports*, Series P-25, No. 1018, 42–87. (Reprinted by permission of Educational Research Service from *Demographic Influence on American Education*, 1990, Arlington, Virginia.)

Enrollment estimates in both public and private schools through the year 2000 are detailed in Table 1.1 and confirm the picture painted in Fig. 1.2: that the first half of the 1990s belongs to younger students, while the second half belongs to older ones. Studies indicate that mobility of the population will cause shifts in school enrollments from state to state. Table 1.2 indicates changes in total school-age population by region for the 1990s and the first five years of the twenty-first century, and points to the West and the South as the two fastest growing parts of the country.

Figure 1.3 **U.S. Population 5 to 17 Years Old and 65 Years Old and Over, for Selected Years: 1975–2020.**

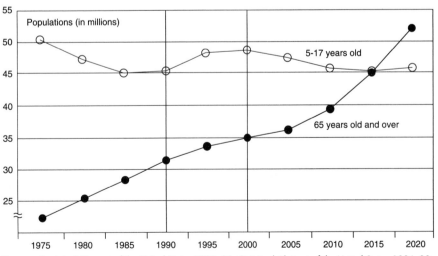

Sources: *Statistical Abstract of the United States 1981*, 28; *Statistical Abstract of the United States 1986*, 28; and U.S. Bureau of the Census, *Current Population Reports*, Series P-25, No. 1018, 38–87. (Reprinted by permission of Educational Research Service from *Demographic Influence on American Education*, 1990, Arlington, Virginia.)

Table 1.1 **Estimates and Projections of Public and Private School Enrollments K–8 and 9–12 Fall 1988; Fall 1992; Fall 2000**

	Total (100s)			Public (1000s)			Private (1000s)		
	K–12[a]	K–8[a]	9–12	K–12[a]	K–8[a]	9–12	K–12[a]	K–8[a]	9–12
1988[b]	45,438	32,426	13,012	40,196	28,390	11,806	5,241	4,036	1,206
1992	47,369	34,481	12,889	41,883	30,189	11,694	5,486	4,292	1,195
1996	49,493	35,161	14,331	43,778	30,785	13,003	5,705	4,376	1,328
2000	49,530	34,741	14,789	43,835	30,417	13,418	5,695	4,324	1,371

[a] Includes most kindergarten and some nursery school enrollment.
[b] Estimate.
Source: *U.S. Department of Education,* Projection of Education Statistics to 2000.

Table 1.2 **Changes in Total School-Age Population, by Region: 1990–2000 and 2000–2005**

	Percent change 1990–2000	Percent change 2000–2005
United States (average)	7.0	–3.0
Northeast	5.8	–4.3
Midwest	0.5	–5.7
South	8.4	–1.7
West	13.1	–1.2

Source: Calculated by ERS from *Current Population Reports,* Series P-25, No. 952; Series P-25, No. 1018; and Series P-25, No. 1017.

The following projections are significant:

• The peak of the current school-age population growth is projected to occur in 1998, when there will be 48.8 million young people, 5 to 17 years old. Of that total, the age breakdown is projected to be as follows:

Age, years	Percent of total, %	Number, millions
5–9	37.0	18.1
10–13	31.6	15.4
14–17	31.4	15.3

• In the year 2000:

The elementary grades will be in a period of population decline.

The middle-school grades will be hitting a peak year, followed by a 10-year decline of 8.4 percent. By the year 2010 there will be 14.1 million middle-school students.

The high-school grades will be up 15.9 percent to 15.3 million students, from an estimated low of 12 million in 1990. Between 2000 and 2010 this group will decline by 3.9 percent, to 13.7 million.

The problem with using these numbers is that they do not necessarily reflect the need for facilities. If, for instance, the entire nation should decide to begin full-day schooling at age 3, the impact on facilities would be tremendous. There is no indication that there will be a decrease in the many special programs now offered in the public schools. With the growing minority populations and the increase in immigration to the United States, it is probable that special programs will increase. The trend to smaller class size also will have a dramatic impact on space needs at schools. All indications point to increasing emphasis on smaller classes. As a result, even with enrollment decreases, more space is likely to be needed.

The Education Construction Market

Construction of educational facilities, like other building types, is sensitive to demographic and economic change. In 1990 education construction reached an all-time high, $14.9 billion for the seventh year in a row. That was an increase of 6 percent over 1989. However, while the amount of construction increased at all levels—elementary through college and university—the rate of increase slowed (see Table 1.3). This was a reflection of the economic recession gripping the country. The need was there, but voters were reluctant to spend the money and increase their taxes. This reluctance, though, further compounds the problem of current space needs and unmet maintenance programs. Deferred maintenance needs will not go away and will have to be met at some point in time.

Table 1.3 **All School Construction, 1986–1990**

Year	Amount, billions $	Increase, %
1986	10.1	—
1987	10.9	07.9
1988	12.5	14.7
1989	14.1	12.8
1990	14.9	06.0

Source: *American School & University Magazine*, 1991.

Table 1.4 breaks down the figures for new construction, additions, and modernization at elementary and secondary schools. The 1990 figures indicate a construction market approaching $10 billion. (These numbers are for actual construction and do not reflect projected need.) Interestingly, additions and modernizations account for a larger part of the total market than new construction. This is a reflection of the aging of facilities and the need to add space to meet smaller class size and special programs, as well as enrollment increases. Some examples of significant modernization projects are illustrated in Chapter 2.

Table 1.4 **School District Construction, Elementary and Secondary Levels (in $000s)**

Construction	1989	1990	Projected, 1991–1993
New	$3,655,816.	$4,110,538	$15,684,000
Additions	2,951,617	3,083,626	11,075,000
Modernization	2,670,118	5,470,997	7,568,000
Total	$9,277,551	$12,665,161	$34,447,000

Source: *American School & University Magazine*, 1991.

Looking at the big picture, it is clear that the 1990s will be a time of steady growth in the education market. From 1991 to 1993 the total for all education construction should be more than $51 billion. The elementary-secondary share of that market is estimated at more than $34 billion, or 66 percent. Guaranteed continued growth over the decade is what most sources predict for the 1990s.

Long-Term Planning a Must

The facility planner today has more information available than at any other time in history and thus should be able to make informed decisions on facility construction. Armed with this information, it is the wise planner who puts any long-range plan in a loose-leaf binder. The future is always subject to change.

As an example, the author remembers one school district that used the best available data to estimate student enrollments, grade organization, and the options available for best accommodating their facilities needs. In less than a year after the completion of the study, it was announced that a major new airport was to be located within this school district. Clearly, such a project would have a dramatic impact. All of the district's projections and estimates had to be totally reworked. In another case, less than four years after a rural school board completed a study, the federal government announced that a proposed supercollider should be located in its district. The giant project, of course, would bring significant numbers of new residents into the district and shatter all of the board's old projections.

In addition to deciding how much to build, school planners must figure out where to build. With Americans being so mobile, the changing ethnic and age composition of communities make it necessary to continually monitor trends. For example, an affluent area near Dallas went through a rather long period of school enrollment stability, followed by decline. Then within a brief two-to-three-year period, the community faced a need for more school space because a large percentage of "empty nesters" was being replaced with families with children. The same situation is now being reported in communities in Chicago, Los Angeles, San Antonio, and other urban areas. Dealing with the cyclical nature of school enrollments is a challenge to planners in all sections of the country. Added to this will be the need for different types of facilities to meet emerging social pressures and concerns such as latch-key children, unmarried mothers and fathers, and single-parent children.

In another example, a school district in the Northeast found a large discrepancy between projected enrollments and actual figures. The reason was a large influx of Hispanic families to the area which had not been taken into consideration. Of the total increase in the Hispanic population, 39 percent consisted of children under age 16. Not surprisingly, between autumn 1981 and autumn 1987, Hispanic children accounted for 85 percent of the total enrollment increase in the district's elementary and junior-high-school classes. If the district had performed an annual analysis of its long-range plan, it would have spotted this discrepancy in its projected enrollments much earlier and would have been able to respond more quickly and effectively.

Lesson: Any long-range plan should be reviewed annually and any necessary adjustments should be made as quickly as possible. This means that plans must be made on more than a "principal's report" indicating his or her estimate of staff and space needs for the coming year. Creating the loose-leaf plan is essential. Luckily, computers make it relatively easy to collect, store, and update data needed to make informed facilities planning decisions. Today it is possible to make planning what it should be—a vital, ongoing exercise that deals with the realities of change.

In some instances the school client—superintendent and board—is experiencing the building process for the first time. As a result, they have no point of reference. They know a house takes six months to build. They do not know that schools can take two to five years. This is a factor that must be understood. Some colleges and universities have attempted to deal with this time-lag problem. For instance, several years ago in New York State, planners proposed "surge space"—space not committed to any academic department but available as temporary classroom space until new construction could be put in place.

There are no easy answers. Today it is not unusual for even medium-sized districts to have a division of facility planning. Smaller districts will either retain outside educational consultants or rely on their architects to assume that responsibility. This awareness of the need for planning has added another dimension to the educational building process. One thing is certain. Gone are the days when the architect was asked to "give us a school with 24 classrooms." School planning today demands specialists.

2

A Brief History of School Design

From the rural one-room schoolhouse to today's specialized facilities, a school's program has always dictated its design. No building type has been more sensitive to changing trends, philosophies, or even fads than the schoolhouse. Some solutions have even prompted others to go beyond the obvious and explore better ways to serve children. Even though yesterday's one-room schoolhouse could easily fit into today's computer room, that in itself does not show progress. In the final analysis, it is the quality of education that the space promotes that is of prime importance.

By surveying major developments in school design over the past 300 years and then focusing on various trends in design from 1940 to 1985, we can show how program has influenced design over time. An illustrated series of 15 case studies designed over the past 50 years indicates the impact of program change on the schoolhouse.

Major Developments: From the One-Room Schoolhouse to the High-School Campus

Education has always been an important aspect of American communities. The first schools in the New England colonies were set up in either private homes or churches. The wealthy hired tutors. The less affluent, if not sending their children to the church school, would intrust the education of their offspring to unmarried or widowed older women who held classes in their own homes. With increases in population came the establishment of subscription schools supported by parental contributions, tuition, land rental fees, and taxes.[1]

The One-Room Schoolhouse—1800 (Even to the Present)

The one-room schoolhouse was the typical school during the early 1800s. One teacher was responsible for the education of all grade levels, hence the design response of one room. The teacher worked with one or two students of the same age or learning ability, making direct supervision possible. After hearing recitations from one or more pupils, the teacher moved to the next individual and repeated the process.

Nineteenth-century grammar schools like the one shown here (opposite) were the first fully graded public schools in the United States.

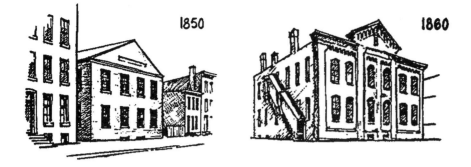

1850   1860

1870

The evolution of school architecture as drawn by C. William Brubaker. Sketches 1850 through 1960 are of schools in Baltimore, while 1970 through 1990 are of schools by Perkins & Will from around the country.

Children were exposed to every lesson. Many times they heard it time after time as older students recited for the teacher in front of the room and then read it themselves from their texts. Students worked at their own pace and were promoted from reader to reader when the teacher believed that each was ready. One student reported that one-room schools provided "the almost unlimited opportunity for the gifted pupil to advance." By having the chance to hear older students recite (after their own assignment was completed), it was not uncommon for children in the fifth or sixth grade (and sometimes even younger) to have mastered everything presented to the seventh and eighth grades. At a much more sophisticated level, this is one of the advantages expressed by exponents of the open-plan school of the 1960s.

As towns grew, their schools often expanded to two rooms, merely adding a duplicate unit. Many of these larger schools were distinguished by a bell tower (reminiscent of the church steeple) and later by facade decorations in the Greek Revival, Queen Anne, or other styles.

As anyone who grew up in a small town remembers, the church and the school were the social centers of the community, serving functions from accommodating town meetings to providing a place for holiday picnics. Even today, in rural communities or ethnic areas of cities, this continues to be the pattern. An historical event that is not too well known is that the Republican Party was organized in 1854 in a little white schoolhouse in Ripon, Wisconsin. In early 1991, a New Hampshire school superintendent who proposed closing a one-room schoolhouse dating back to the 1840s was the target of criticism from parents who opposed children being moved to a more "impersonal school setting." These historic schools may seem quaintly attractive when viewed as part of a restored village, but back in their heyday, they were often dirty, noisy and ill suited to the process of education. Nevertheless, the one-room schoolhouse has been romanticized in Western novels, movies, and television production and was ideally suited to the rural makeup of the country during much of the nineteenth century. In fact, as of 1990 there were still 729 one-teacher public schools in operation in the United States.[2]

The Lancastrian School System—1806–1840

As the country became more urbanized, education needed to respond. One teacher no longer had a small group of 5 to 15 students. In the Lancastrian school (named for English educator Joseph Lancaster), the teacher grilled a group of 50 leaders, students who accepted the role of monitors. Each monitor was responsible for supervising the recitations and drills of 10 pupils. Thus, one teacher theoretically could teach 500 students. To work, the Lan-

castrian school system, with roots in England, was almost militarylike in operation. The design response was a room 50 by 100 feet with rows of benches for groups of 10 pupils and their monitors.

Order was the byword. Noise was kept to a minimum. Those who have studied Cotton Mather and Jonathan Edwards can understand why this strict organization by age and achievement was widely accepted during this period. Fortunately, the approach was short-lived.

A Lancasterian school in operation, from *Public Education in the United States,* by Ellwood P. Cubberley. Copyright 1934, 1919, by Houghton Mifflin Company. Used with permission.

Lancastrian schools spread quickly and disappeared almost as fast. By 1840 they had become things of the past. But the system had made a lasting mark for which it deserves to be remembered. Until this time education had been a slow, expensive process because it had been carried out on an individual basis or in very small groups. By establishing the principle of group instruction at a low cost and by orienting people toward the idea of education for the many rather than the few, Lancaster's schools paved the way for free, public, tax-supported schools such as we have today.

The Transitional School—1840–1850

The free, graded school, however, did not arrive overnight. It had to go through a step-by-step process of evolution. An important step was the unification of the separate reading and writing schools which functioned independently of each other, although situated in the same building. The separate schools were autonomous units; the teacher in each school was the

ruler of his or her own kingdom. This domain consisted of a large classroom with a smaller, satellite room attached on one side. The master would divide the work with an assistant, who, while instructing the group, would hear individual recitation in the smaller annex to the main room.

After unification of these separate schools, the final step was sorting and grouping the children by age into seven, eight, or nine grades with a separate teacher for each grade and a system of promotion from one grade to the next with a corresponding progression of subject matter.

The ultimate organizational step came about naturally, as the course of instruction slowly expanded with such subjects as history, grammar, composition, and even bookkeeping added over time. Moreover, by the mid–nineteenth century textbooks were in common use, the school term had been lengthened, and the years of schooling had been increased. The graded school was a child of the cities. Rural areas continued for many years to lump all their young hopefuls together in one ungraded collection.

The Graded Elementary School—1848–Present

As the delivery of education became more sophisticated—expansion of subjects, extended use of textbooks, lengthening of the school year, and so on—it was a natural step to sort the students into groupings by age. The design profession responded. It is generally accepted that the first fully graded public school in the United States was Boston's Quincy Grammar School built in 1848. The design response was a four-story building with a basement and an attic. The building was designed to house 660 students. The first three floors had a series of four classrooms opening onto a common corridor. Each classroom housed 55 students in rooms measuring 31 by 26 feet. There is no apparent reason for the dimension of the room other than the maximum number of people (55) that could be accommodated in the space. Each classroom had an attached closet. Individual desks—an important innovation—were bolted to the floor, seven rows of them, eight to a row, less one seat in the back row made necessary by a structural column. The top floor was a large assembly hall with benches to seat the entire student body. An administrative office was located on the first floor.

The education delivered in the classrooms was essentially the same. The pupil sat at a desk, listened to the teacher, and participated only when called on to stand and recite. The same floor plan with its 800- to 900-square-foot self-contained classroom is still the most common arrangement today. The total plan—design response—is essentially the same, although the facade varies according to the local community's or architect's preference.

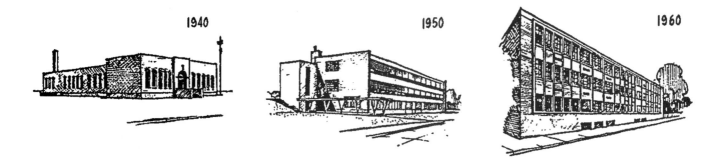

1940   1950   1960

Educational theorists such as John Dewey and William James began to question this method of education on the grounds that a child is not a sponge soaking up information. Rather, they contended, education should be based on a broader concept as an integral part of the life process, of learning by doing through creative participation. Their questions resulted in a radical change in the educational process. Discussion, evaluation, investigation, and self-expression were terms that began to be heard. Class sizes began to get smaller, shrinking to 40, 35, or 30 children. The era of regimented instruction was fast disappearing, although its vestiges can still be seen in some schools today.

During this period, new subject matter was added such as geography and science. Group activities—for example, building models and running science experiments—replaced the passive activities of the past. The influence on interior design was dramatic. Inside, desks were unbolted and more space was granted to accommodate more active students. Storage needs became an urgent design requirements. Kindergartens were added to the public schools. The first public kindergarten opened in St. Louis in 1873. At the other end of the elementary grade level, "manual training" classes began to appear. Boys took metal or woodworking classes and girls, "home arts." The total design response was larger classrooms, more storage space, and even more utilities for science experiments. Rooms designed for music—both vocal and instrumental—and gymnasiums made their appearance as well.

Improvements in such schools were substantial during the early twentieth century, particularly in health and safety factors. Heating, lighting, toilet facilities, eating facilities, space per pupil, and fire safety advanced considerably. But architecture stood still. Whether architects applied Gothic or Spanish Colonial, Greek Revival or Victorian faces to these schools, they were essentially clusters of one-room schools, stacked up for two or three stories, to which a cavernous gymnasium and auditorium were often added along with a few other specialized spaces such as library, office, and cafeteria. Despite local autonomy in school matters these buildings are startling in their nationwide similarity. In the 1930s and early 1940s the historical gingerbread often disappeared leaving a brick box with holes for windows in a style which can only be described as neutered.

There were notable exceptions to these monumental buildings with their impressive entries and halls and their depressing rooms. Frank Lloyd Wright's Hillsdale Home School in Spring Green, Wisconsin, designed at the turn of the century, and Dwight Perkins' Carl Schurz High School in Chicago, built in 1910, were two exceptions that pointed the way toward better space planning, a scale more appropriate to the younger generation,

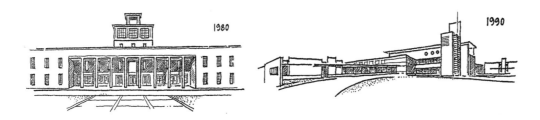

1980   1990

and a freedom from the dictates of historical eclecticism. Such exceptions, though, were rare until just before World War II, when an explosion of architectural creativity hit the field of schoolhouse design.

Evolution of the Junior and Senior High School

It was a natural progression to add grades to the education system. In the 1860s there were only about 300 high schools. Since the Kalamazoo Decision of 1874, when the Supreme Court of the United States ruled that free schools maintained by locally imposed taxes were legal, the high school had become an extension of the elementary school. As the public demanded greater educational opportunities, the number of high schools grew. By 1900 there were more than 6000 high schools throughout the country.

While schools for young adolescents have a short history, the earlier secondary schools that appeared between 1850 and 1860 had the advantage of building on the history of the lower grades. The evolution of the high school to the institution we know today includes the introduction of physical education as a response to the attention given European athletes who performed at the 1893 Columbia Exposition.

By 1900 high schools were offering college preparation courses, vocational shops, and some clerical-related subjects. At about the same time, instrumental music was recognized as an extracurricular subject. Vocal music had been accepted early in the nineteenth century. By 1910 general science courses were introduced into high schools. In 1917 the federal government encouraged vocational training programs. The next year, 1918, physical education received increased attention after one-third of the men drafted for service in World War I were rejected as unfit. Other subjects such as drama, journalism, health, and foreign languages have been added over the years, but basic subject areas have not changed much since about 1920.

What to do with the early adolescent seems to always have been a concern. In 1910 the junior high school appeared as a response to the question. The schools were usually organized to house grades 7 to 8 or 7 to 9. The first junior high schools were established early in the century for justifiable reasons that almost immediately became irrelevant. At the turn of the century almost two-thirds of all pupils quit school before grade 9. Educators rationalized that those leaving school after grade 9 should be prepared to support themselves so the curriculum was organized to include some secondary education and a little vocational training. As a result, junior high school became terminal education for some and an introduction to high school for others. As time went by, the junior high school took on the rigid departmentalization and extracurricular fanfare of the high school. Today, most junior high schools include grades 6 through 8. Where this organization varies, the reason is in response to space needs caused by bulges in grade enrollments, not because of educational philosophy.

Junior-high-school education continues to be a topic of debate among educators. In the foreword of a 1989 report released by the Carnegie Corporation's Council on Adolescent Development[3] it is stated that young adolescents have been largely ignored in the recent surge of educational reform. It says that as currently organized, these middle grades constitute an arena of casualties—damaging to both students and teachers. Negative forces identified include massive, impersonal schools, unconnected and seemingly irrelevant curricula, and a lack of health-care and counseling services.

The report is having an impact and is being used by planners as they program middle-school facilities. The commission recommended the creation of smaller learning environments. It suggested that large schools be organized into "houses" of 200 to 300, but no more than 500 students. The report further recommended that teachers and students be organized into teams. The report strongly recommended the assignment of an adult adviser for every student. These and other suggestions have obvious facility and space implications.

Recent Trends in School Design— 1940–1985

A qualitative leap in school design took place in the years leading up to 1985 precisely because architects and educators responded to changing needs and philosophies in program. Certainly, the most influential design was Crow Island School, built in 1940 in Winnetka, Illinois. This small elementary school set off a quiet revolution with its organization of classrooms into wings, each with its own identity. Providing classrooms with direct access to outdoor yards and designing rooms with a child's perspective in mind were other radical innovations.

Many more changes followed as architects scrambled to build schools to accommodate the postwar baby boom and keep up with changing social conditions. The need for flexibility led to the systems approach to building schools and then to the open plan. At about the same time, magnet schools were developed as a response to segregation in education. The renovation of existing schools and the addition of portable classroom wings soon developed as typical solutions to the need to expand educational facilities. When school enrollments began dropping in the 1970s, many school districts had to deal with surplus space. Throughout the country, many local governments sold off unneeded schools. Some of these old buildings came down, while others were converted to alternative uses such as shopping malls, office buildings, and even apartments. Community-schools emerged when localities demanded that buildings be operated from early in the morning until late at night for the benefit of people of all ages. Fads such as fallout shelters in school basements, windowless classrooms, stock plans, and classes on buses, boats, planes, and helicopters have all come and gone. But some important approaches to school design have been pioneered in the postwar period and will continue to influence educational architecture. Five such approaches are described below.

The Systems Approach to School Buildings

The early to mid-1960s was a time of rapid growth, which spawned the systems approach to building schools. In 1962 the School Construction Systems Development (SCSD) project in California focused on two primary needs of school buildings: built-in flexibility to keep pace with rapidly and unpredictably changing user needs, and an improved learning environment. SCSD was based on the belief that building systems could streamline the process of designing and erecting new schools. It brought together on site eight or 10 prefabricated assembly systems including structure, partitions, lighting, and ceiling, and integrated them into a single process. The idea was to create a building that would be readily responsive to changing space needs. SCSD produced various projects in California, Florida, and Canada. Many aspects of the systems approach are in general use today.

Magnet Schools

A citywide institution that uses a special curriculum to attract pupils from all neighborhoods and all ethnic groups, the magnet school was a response to the civil rights movement of the 1960s. Dr. Nolan Estes, then superintendent of the Dallas school system, pointed out that the concept of the magnet school was actually not new. A technical trade school established in Dallas in 1929, for example, drew students from throughout the district. Some experts might say the late-nineteenth century reading, writing, Latin, and English schools were, indeed, magnet schools according to the following definition by Estes:[4] "They bring together students of different races and backgrounds who have common interests and goals, but for educational reasons rather than for the simple exercise of mixing bodies. In a magnet-school setting, racial and socioeconomic barriers come tumbling down more rapidly than they do in settings where there may be an equal mix of races, but where there may also exist an isolating distance between these races." In fact, magnet schools were the second generation of the alternative school movement. During the 1960s and early 1970s educators, especially in urban schools, wrestled with ways to meet court-mandated school integration. In Dallas, for example, a federal court ordered the opening of four centrally located magnet schools: the Arts Magnet High School, the Business and Management Center, the High School for Health Professions, and the Transportation Institute.

Today magnet schools are an established and accepted part of the educational scene. It is unusual for there not to be at least one magnet school in a city school district. While most innovative programs have historically begun in the elementary school, the reverse has been true with magnets. But there are exceptions. For instance, in Kansas City there are elementary schools concentrating on physical and biological sciences and mathematics, computer science, and even classical Greek and environmental science. The arts have been a favorite subject for magnet schools. In Louisiana, the New Orleans Center for the Creative Arts has received international acclaim and

New York City's School for the Performing Arts was the subject of "Fame," a popular motion picture and television series. Today there are some 5000 magnet schools in the United States.

Found Space

In the late 1960s and early 1970s, school districts could not keep up with growing school populations. School districts in all parts of the country went prospecting for space and found it in unused factories, supermarkets, and shopping centers, practically any place (including a public bathhouse in Boston). Often the school district was able to acquire this real estate for a relatively low price and the cost of renovation was usually less, often dramatically less, than site acquisition and construction of new buildings. But the most important factor was getting needed space in a hurry.

Did found spaces work as schools? In most cases, the answer was "yes." The teachers and students at these facilities often reported that they felt more freedom to adapt the spaces to fit their needs. The restrictions, real or imagined, for changing interiors in a traditional school were removed. Allegiance to these schools was so strong in some cases that when new facilities replaced the found space, a sense of loss was reported. In Louisiana, where the New Orleans Center for the Creative Arts is scheduled to leave its found space for a new facility, more than one user expressed concern that they would lose some of the freedom they now have. Part of this can be contributed to the feeling of camaraderie that occurs when a group has to work together to overcome adversity. But part is, undoubtedly, due to the feeling that the user can have an important role in shaping his or her environment.

The Open-Plan School

Probably no educational philosophy caused more controversy during the past 30 years than the open-plan school. The concept burst on the scene in the 1960s and by 1970 open-plan schools were operating in all parts of the country. The concept was heralded as the answer to the need for flexibility. The open plan promised flexibility to change space almost at will; to adapt to large, small, and individual group instruction; and to react to the needs of the teacher and the student. Not only were new schools built to house the open-plan concept, but the walls in existing schools were also knocked down to accommodate the new approach.

The SCSD schools were ideal for those planning to build with the open concept. The modular system permitted walls to be arranged in practically any configuration desired. This was the period of freedom of expression, the recognition of the individual. And the open-plan school was the educator's reaction. To some, an open-plan school meant vast, wide-open areas of undivided space. Others envisioned it as a group of classroom clusters or pods which are open within themselves but not to each other.

Open-plan schools represented a commitment to the belief that education is dynamic—that change is inevitable. The essence of their value was that they released those who use them to "do their own thing." If the program was traditional at first, it could still fit into the open-plan school merely by having interior partitions installed. Or the program could be experimental from the start. Whether traditional or way-out, the educational program was bound to change, figured proponents of the open plan. When it does change, so will the school, painlessly and economically.

Those who favored more open-plan schools were commited to far more than the concept of change in educational content and techniques. They believed that children learn more effectively in open space. They believed that self-direction and self-motivation will prepare a student better for additional learning and for a fuller, more satisfying life. They believed that learning in the open-plan environment would lead the individual to be more innovative, self-assured, intelligent, and understanding. As one report stated:[5] "While open plan schooling may seem an innovation, it carries on the tradition of the one-room schoolhouse, expanded to accommodate 1,000 students. The concept also attempts to instill in students the quality of independence that we admire in our forefathers."

Open-plan high schools followed open-plan elementary schools by several years. The design came into use at the beginning of the school process and worked its way up because it is easier to change the learning style of children who haven't had eight or nine years of experience in another tradition.

It was not easy, however, to change those who were to be in charge: teachers. Because young teachers have always been trained to look forward to the time when they would get their own private classroom—their own domain where they can close the door and be in charge of the learning of the 30 or so eager youngsters—many of them resisted or resented the open plan.

Then in the mid to late 1970s educators started putting the walls back up. Teachers had already begun to use bookcases and file cabinets to create more traditional classroom settings. As one observer said: "They're putting their wagons in a circle to protect themselves from attacks."

Today, there are few open-plan schools. In some of those remaining, the addition of walls has resulted in awkward interior environments. The open plan's demise can be attributed to teachers refusing to work in the environment, making certain it did not work, returning to educational basics and therefore returning to a more traditional classroom.

Community Schools

In the 1970s the concept of community-schools emerged. "The slash mark: community/schools [community-schools], does more than separate two words," wrote Larry Molloy in the preface to his book on the subject.[6] "It distinguishes two entirely different concepts in the use of educational facilities. Community schools (without the slash) simply open their doors to the public after school hours. Community/schools do not differentiate between school hours and public hours because the entire building is operated for the benefit of people of all ages in the community and is paid for and operated by educational and other public service agencies," added Molloy.

Such schools have appeared in all parts of the country. The John F. Kennedy School and Community Center in Atlanta provides for a middle-school program plus services and programs for more than 20 agencies ranging from legal aid and senior citizens to social security and welfare casework. The Whitmer Human Resources Center in Pontiac, Michigan, replaced four elementary schools and includes office space for 10 community agencies. The Thomas Jefferson, Jr. High School and Community Center in Arlington, Virginia, is open from 6 a.m. to midnight, seven days a week. Junior-high-school students mix with adults and preschool tots. "All ages eat together in the dining area, and the school generally closes with adult and university-extension classes moving into the spaces vacated by junior high students," reported Molloy.

A force behind the Thomas Jefferson facility was assistant superintendent Joseph Ringers. "More and more governmental units are turning to the sensible solutions offered by interagency programs based in community/ schools because school facilities can meet many of the needs," he wrote.[7] "School vehicles and equipment can be used at no deterioration of service to school children. Educational programs can profit from the community/school programs which bring people of diverse age and social groups together under a common roof."

Most of the early community/schools are still active and, as should be expected, have evolved as community needs have changed. In some instances, such as at the Pontiac school, traditional educational programs have replaced many of the service agencies because of enrollment increases. But the movement is alive. Texas Governor Ann Richards in a 1991 appearance before the State Board of Education advocated locating social service agencies in schools "where the people who need the services are located." Governor Richards said she saw no reason why a person should have to leave his or her neighborhood and journey downtown to a high-rise office building to get social services.

Notes

1. Educational Facilities Laboratories, *The Cost of a Schoolhouse,* EFL, 1960, pp. 18–28.

2. Andrew Gulliford, *America's Country Schools,* Preservation Press, 1990, p. 278.

3. Carnegie Council on Adolescent Development, *Turning Points: Preparing American Youth for the 21st Century,* June 1989, pp. 12–14.

4. Nolan Estes and Donald Waldrip, *Magnet Schools: Legal and Practical Implications,* New Century Education Corporation, 1978.

5. Educational Facilities Laboratories, *Five Open Plan High Schools,* EFL, 1973, p. 6.

6. Larry Molloy, *Community/School: Sharing the Space and the Action,* Educational Facilities Laboratories, 1973, p. 3.

7. Joseph Ringers, *Community/Schools and Interagency Programs,* Pendell Publishing Company, 1976, p. 5.

Portfolio of Landmark Schools

If Crow Island School was the bridge between the past and the present, traffic across that bridge has been heavy. From the 1950s to 1985, hundreds of distinguished buildings have been designed to house the nation's schools. Fifteen case studies illustrated in this chapter show some of the major trends discussed earlier. The projects were designed by a few architects who took the time to collaborate with educators before putting pencil to paper. While many have undergone changes over the years in response to new program demands, most will continue to serve as excellent places for education for many years to come.

Each classroom has direct access to its own outdoor space.

Brickwork detail.

Crow Island Elementary School, 1940
Winnetka, Illinois

Perkins, Wheeler & Will with Eliel and
Eero Saarinen, architects

34,800 square feet

350 students

For over 50 years now Crow Island
Elementary School has stood as a
landmark of collaboration between
architect, client, and user. The most
honored school building of the past
half century, Crow Island began with
the progressive educational program
of a young superintendent named
Carleton W. Washburne and became
a reality only after an extended
period of listening, analysis, and discussion among educators, teachers,
and designers. By the time Crow
Island was finished, the participants
in the process had swept away all
traces of the Victorian schoolhouse;
gone were the imposing scale, formal
architecture, and rigid organization
of classroom cells within a two- or
three-story box. In their place, Crow
Island offered a residential scale and
an informal (but carefully considered) plan that divided classrooms
into separate wings, each with its
own identity.

A one-story brick structure
with a clock tower anchoring the
composition slightly off center, Crow
Island is a welcoming rather than
intimidating presence—a radical
notion in 1940. A broad set of stairs
at the entrance and generous
amounts of glazing help maintain
the relaxed tone for the entire building. Window seats, 9-foot ceilings
(instead of the more traditional, but
less intimate, 12 feet), and direct
access to the outdoors from every
classroom remind children that this
building was designed for them.

One participant whose voice
was heard during the design process
was the "creative activities" teacher
who wrote a letter to the architects
expressing her feelings on the purpose of materials. She wrote, "The
building must not be too beautiful,
lest it be a place for children to keep

and not one for them to use. The materials must be those not easily marred, and permitting of some abuse. The finish and settings must form a harmonious background with honest child effort and creation, not one which will make children's work seem crude. Above all the school must be child-like, not what adults think of children. It must be warm, personal, and intimate, that it shall be to thousands of children through the years 'my school.' "

That it is. At Crow Island, common rose-colored brick is used on both the exterior and interior, while trim is redwood on the outside and Ponderosa pine treated with wax on the inside. The architects enhanced

Main entrance facade is anchored by a modern clock tower.

Furniture for the school was designed by the architects.

the effect of these natural materials by bringing generous amounts of natural light inside. Both halls and classrooms combine skylights with artificial sources. Another unusual touch found more often in residential than institutional buildings are the three fireplaces: one in the "pioneer room" where early American cooking demonstrations are held, another in a reception corridor, and a third in what was originally the library and is now a conference and meeting room.

In both 1956 and 1991 Crow Island was named one of the most important buildings completed in America during the preceding 100 years in polls conducted by *Architectural Record*. Among its other honors, the school has received the American Institute of Architects' 25-year award and was designated a national historic landmark in 1990.

A typical classroom.

Hillsdale High School, 1955
San Mateo, California

John Lyon Reid & Partners (now Reid & Tarics), architect

231,000 square feet

1750 students

Built on a modular system, Hillsdale High was designed for flexibility. Detachable exterior panels, modular light and ventilation systems, and movable partitions all make changes in the building quite easy. And indeed, the school has been rearranged several times over the years. In the early 1960s an additional bay was added to the building and part of the interior was remodeled using newly designed glass block that helps diffuse light.

As educational concepts changed over the years, so did Hillsdale. When the open plan became a popular idea in the 1970s, the school took down many of its interior partitions and encouraged team teaching. And when the demand for open teaching spaces subsided later on, the walls went back up.

The architects for the project even considered how the school might be converted to an alternative use sometime in the future. As a result, they designed Hillsdale with an eye toward its possible conversion into a manufacturing or business facility, should student enrollment decline. Although Hillsdale has remained a school, the architects did a study for the U.S. Postal Service in the late 1970s to convert a similar project into a mail-handling facility.

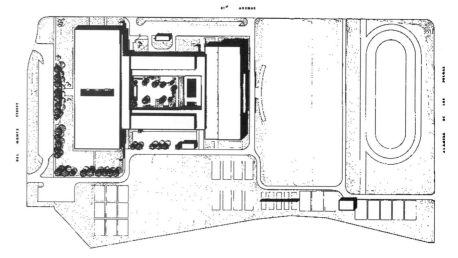

Site plan.

Exterior showing the school's structural bays.

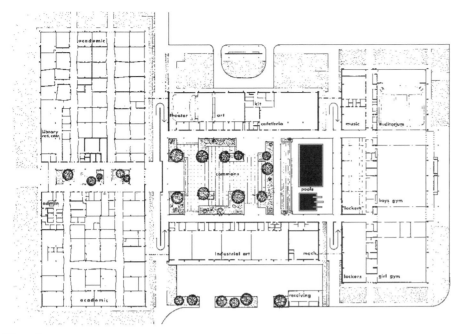

Floor plan.

View of central courtyard.

The University of Chicago Laboratory High School, 1960
Chicago, Illinois

Perkins & Will and J. Lee Jones, associate architects

Eero Saarinen, design consultant

96,000 square feet

800 students

With the Soviet Union's launch of *Sputnik* in 1957 and the beginning of the space race, the United States began a crash program to strengthen its teaching of the sciences. The University of Chicago Laboratory High School was one of a number of new facilities dedicated to teaching a new generation of future-oriented Americans. As a result, the design of the school was relentlessly experimental, adopting the latest building products, technical systems, and amenities.

Four different types of removable walls were installed and evaluated. All classrooms were wired for transmitting and receiving closed-circuit television, and each had its own film projector, screen, and light dimmers. Another new teaching facility was the foreign-language lab equipped with study carrels and individual headphones—an innovation that would eventually sweep through the country. On top of the building, the architects built a weather station for meteorology instruction.

A four-story structure, the school completes a quadrangle with three other buildings. Although modern in every sense, the structure is clad in limestone and reflective dark glass that harmonizes with the Gothic architecture of its neighbors.

The high school forms one edge of a quadrangle and harmonizes with its Neogothic neighbors.

View from the quadrangle.

Language laboratory.

Movable partitions could open one classroom to another.

**Dundee Elementary
School,** 1962
Greenwich, Connecticut

Perkins & Will, architect

71,500 square feet

550 students

In the early 1960s educators talked a
great deal about team teaching. As
the name implies, the approach organized pupils and teachers into teams,
varying in size from individual
groups of 20 or 30 students to large
"clans" of up to 150.

A leader in the field of team
teaching, Dundee Elementary used a
combination of small project rooms
for individualized learning, clusters
of classrooms with movable partitions, and grand spaces for large
gatherings. The school is a split-level
design on three levels making maximum use of its 14-acre site. From the

Gymnasium.

The school fits into its wooded suburban setting.

exterior, the school is a pleasant-looking facility that blends into a residential area of Greenwich. On the inside the school takes advantage of its sophisticated system of movable walls. Operated electronically with a 90-second cutoff time, the walls are activated by pressurized air from a central compressor. When retracted, the walls disappear behind permanent partitions. To free up classrooms for team teaching, almost all teaching materials are stored in hallways rather than in the classrooms themselves.

Storage units in hallways free classrooms for team teaching.

Electronically operated movable walls can turn lecture rooms into an assembly hall.

Valley Winds Elementary School, 1964
St. Louis County, Missouri

John A. Shaver, architect

43,246 square feet

660 students

A spiral radiating from its center to form three concentric rings, Valley Winds Elementary was nicknamed "the snail school" even before it was completed. The school's inner core is divided between a curriculum-planning center for teachers on the upper level and an electronic "nerve center" and production area on the lower level. The spiral just outside this core contains an instructional-materials center, a children's theater, and a suite of administrative offices. The outer spiral contains the equivalent of 20 wedge-shaped classrooms. To complete the snail effect, the architect designed a covered play shelter that flows from the outer "shell" and forms an appropriately shaped "head."

A year after the school opened, Architect John Shaver said, "The children's theater is probably the most successful space in the building. This simple carpeted area has terraces for seating, and three acting platforms."

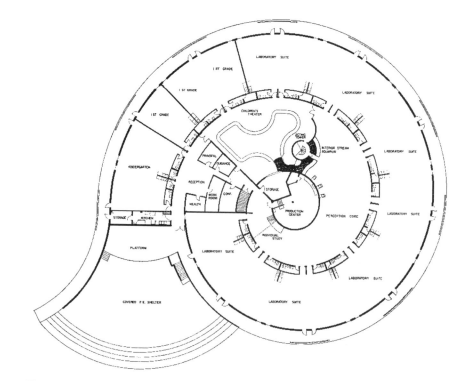

Floor plan.

No one ever wonders why it is called the "snail school."

No furniture is used. Though we should have been aware of this fact, we failed to recognize, during planning, that small children enjoy the opportunity of being informal."

Although the school's snail shape at first seems arbitrary, it turns out to be an efficient way of enclosing space. Because it required about 25 percent less exterior surface than a rectangular building containing the same amount of square footage would have, the school reduced building costs. Shaver's plan also eliminated long corridors, which usually take up about 20 percent of floor space in a conventional building. Teachers and students have found the free-flowing plan well suited to the school's flexible educational program.

Beyond its purely functional aspects, the snail school also works because its whimsical form inspires children to reexamine their environment. By subverting the standard image of a building, Shaver's design encourages students to question conventions and think for themselves. One seven-year-old expressed it best: "Is this really a school?"

Children's theater has terraces for sitting and three acting platforms.

P.S. 219, 1965
New York City

Caudill Rowlett Scott (now CRSS Architects, Inc.), architect

575 students

First planned for Port Arthur, Texas, this dome-shaped school design found its way to Queens, New York, after the original school district's bond issue failed to get the necessary approvals. Architect William Caudill then showed the unusual design to Harold Gores, then head of Educational Facilities Laboratories, an influential research center funded by the Ford Foundation. Soon thereafter Gores convinced the New York City Board of Education that a domed school was exactly the kind of show-

The school's domed structure is evident indoors as well as outdoors.

Interior spaces flow into one another.

case project it was looking to build on a site near the upcoming World's Fair in Flushing Meadows. Although the school wasn't completed in time for the 1964 Fair, it attracted a great deal of attention on its own.

Like many other innovative schools of the period, P.S. 219 featured a flexible plan that allowed teachers to arrange students in groups of varying sizes. The school's domed three-story interior was, indeed, perfectly suited for the less structured method of teaching popular at the time.

The shallow dome catches the spirit of the 1964 World's Fair in nearby Flushing Meadows.

Uninterrupted interior space can be divided with shelves and furniture.

The Lamplighter School, 1969
Dallas, Texas

O'Neil Ford & Associates, architect

25,000 square feet

350 students

George Zimbel

When approaching the entrance to the Lamplighter School, the first thing one notices is the inscription over the door that declares, "A student is not a vessel to be filled, but a lamp to be lighted." While it is not unusual to find such lofty expressions over schoolhouse doors, it *is* unusual to find a school where everyone actually believes in its message and incorporates it in their work.

Dedicated to a K–4 (kindergarten-through-grade-4) program that emphasizes both academic and nonacademic areas, the school offers a nontraditional environment for learning. For example, animals roam freely on the school's small farm and children are encouraged to learn by caring for them. Another unique feature is the requirement that all students learn French. By the time students reach the fourth grade, they have learned enough of the language to produce a play in French (with translations prepared for monolingual parents).

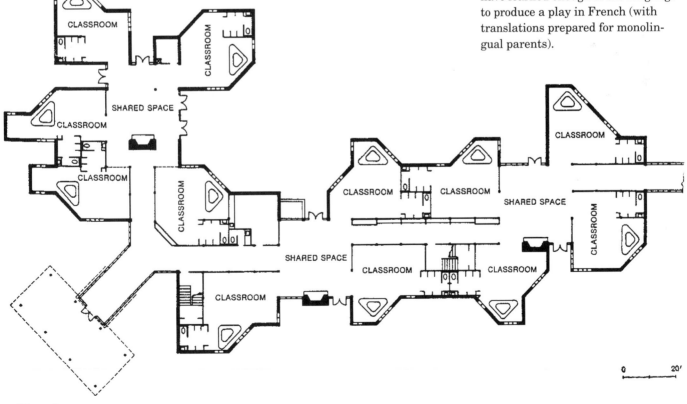

Floor plan.

Located off a busy North Dallas street, Lamplighter is a true oasis of learning. Designed to be residential in scale, the school is a two-story structure in which the second level is used by parents, teachers, and visitors as a viewing area into classrooms below. Large windows of one-way glass overlook each of the classrooms, making observation and explanations possible without disrupting the children. The school's tight L-shaped plan maximizes the usage of nearly every square foot of space. In fact, even corridors are used for shared activities and teaching, making the entire school hum with activity.

Instead of traditional rectilinear classrooms, Lamplighter features irregularly shaped rooms, all of which include informal learning pits, individual restrooms, and custom-designed furniture. Special storage units in which each child has his or her own open cubicle don't raise many eyebrows today, but were considered innovative in 1969.

A great success with both children and parents, Lamplighter continues to have a waiting list for new admissions. In the early 1990s the school did some remodeling, adding a permanent library and other support facilities. But the architects were instructed not to change the school's unusual plan or tamper with its successful spaces. As a result, the school's environment has stayed much the same—with just a little more space to help teachers light a few more lamps.

Recent addition to the Lamplighter school recalls the design of the original building.

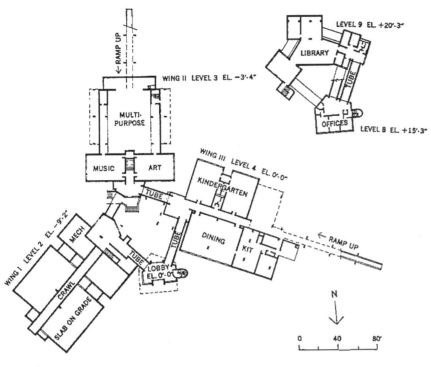

Floor plan.

L. Francis Smith Elementary School,
1970
Columbus, Indiana
Johansen & Bhavnani, architect
50,000 square feet
485 students

A classic example of the kind of innovative educational programs encouraged in the late 1960s and early 1970s, the L. Francis Smith Elementary School purposefully breaks with tradition. To reflect the experimental, loosely structured teaching methods of the school, architect John Johansen designed a building that engages and challenges students with new forms, bright colors, industrial materials, and an unusual plan. No one ever confuses this building with a stodgy old school from a previous era.

Like many of the best public buildings erected in Columbus, Indiana, over the last three and a half decades, L. Francis Smith Elementary was a beneficiary of the Cummins Engine Foundation's corporate largesse—a standing offer to pick up the fees of innovative architects.

Main entrance.

The school's most prominent features are the enclosed ramps or "tubes" that emanate from a central core and lead to the three classroom wings. Made of self-supporting corrugated metal and lined completely on the inside with carpeting, the tubes bring the school alive with a sense of motion. While shared spaces such as a covered play yard, administrative facilities, a resource center, and a dining hall sit on the ground floor, classrooms occupy the upper portion of the building. Each classroom wing is a series of light-metal boxes and can be expanded by the addition of more boxes. Reflecting the period's enthusiasm for educational experimentation, four of each wing's six classrooms were designed for team teaching and all of the classrooms were equipped with closed-circuit television for audiovisual instruction.

View of central courtyard.

Enclosed ramps or "tubes" connect various floor levels.

Greenwich High School, 1970
Greenwich, Connecticut
Reid & Tarics Associates, architect
368,000 square feet
2500 to 3000 students

When lists of best academic high schools are compiled, Greenwich High is always included in the top 5 or 10. This commitment to excellence is as apparent in the school's architecture as it is in the students' SAT (Scholastic Aptitude Test) scores. When this school was featured in the November 1971 issue of *Architectural Record*,[1] the editors wrote, "Rarely do public high schools have the qualities which abound in the new Greenwich High School. . . . [The] architectural solution saved trees and rock outcroppings, preserved the pond as a natural biological resource, and used all of these attributes to provide the kind of places, indoors and out whose connotations of building with landscape, and vice versa, remains indelible in memory years after graduation."

A pond was preserved as a natural resource.

The architects retained as many existing trees and natural features as possible.

The school's plan is in response to an education program calling for the entire student body (capacity 3000) to be divided into four semiautonomous "houses." Each house functions as a "school within a school," administered by its own staff and equipped with space for teachers and guidance counselors.

The site presented several challenges in the design process. Because the school was located in a residential area, the architects designed it as a group of several buildings rather than as one large structure. Early in the design process, participants agreed that a picturesque pond located on the site should be preserved as a natural biological resource. The architects then oriented science laboratories toward the pond but kept the rest of the school far enough away to safeguard

Stairway in the student center.

The student center is the focal point for the entire school and can hold up to 2000 people.

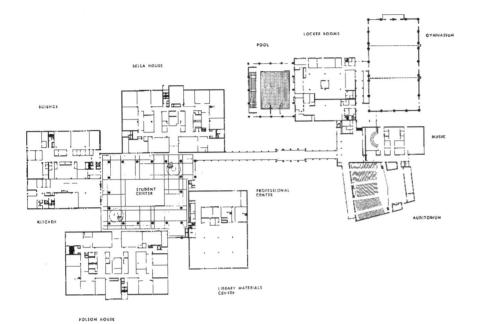

First floor.

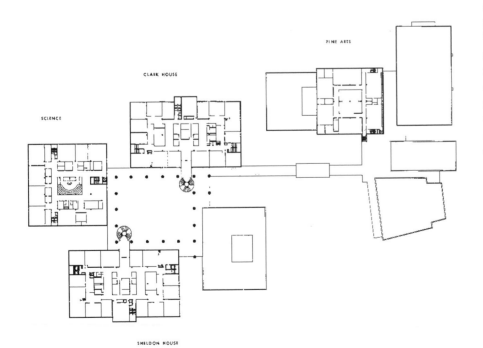

Second floor.

this refuge area. Maintaining an ecologically sensitive approach throughout the design process, the architects located the school's buildings and courtyards around an existing array of trees and plants, carefully blending architecture and nature.

In accordance with program requirements, two building clusters evolved: a northern cluster with specialized functions such as arts and physical education, and a southern group with more general academic functions. In the academic cluster, four buildings surround a two-story student center. Two of these buildings contain common facilities such as library, administration, and science center. The other two buildings contain the four academic houses, each located on its own floor and organized as a series of suites. Each suite contains traditional classrooms as well as small-group and individual study spaces. Each house also has a large-group instruction space that can accommodate up to 100 students. Science facilities are organized in a similar manner, with large-group areas and individual and small-group study spaces.

In the placement and design of the student center, the architects created a grand space that serves as the focal point for the entire high school. The center functions as both a dining area and a social space for large meetings and concerts. Able to accommodate up to 2000 people, the student center brings all of the students together as citizens of the school. Similarly, the library resource center, conveniently located off the student center, serves as the educational heart of the school.

The school's exterior materials—mainly brick, concrete, and wood—were chosen for their inherent beauty and because they complement the site's natural features. The materials have only improved with age. Metal-alloy fascias at the top of the buildings' brick walls, for example, require no maintenance and have continued to develop a rich deep-gray color over the years.

Note

1. "Greenwich High School," *Architectural Record,* November 1971, pp. 133–138.

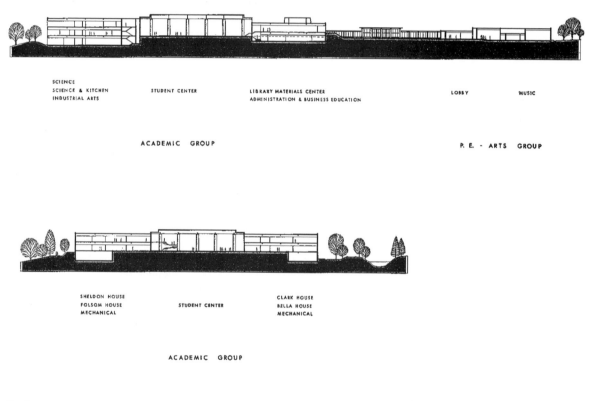

Sections.

Mt. Healthy Elementary School, 1972
Columbus, Indiana

Hardy Holzman Pfeiffer Associates,
architect

David B. Hill & Associates, associate
architect

50,000 square feet

660 students

Bold geometry reflects a new way of organizing educational spaces.

The first open-plan school built in Columbus, Indiana—a town famous for its innovative architecture—Mt. Healthy Elementary broke a lot of new ground when it opened in 1972. One observer wrote:[1] "It is certainly one of the best centers for informal learning so far built in the United States."

Although high-powered architects such as John Carl Warnecke, Norman Fletcher (TAC), Gunnar Birkirts, Edward L. Barnes, John Johansen, Elliot Noyes, and Mitchell/Giurgola had already designed interesting schools for Columbus, all of these facilities had followed fairly traditional educational programs. By the time Hardy Holzman Pfeiffer came along, the Columbus School Board was ready to experiment with some of the latest concepts in education.

HHPA responded with a visually exciting design that organizes

Multilevel clusters of 180 students each are expressed on the school's exterior.

the school into three multilevel clusters of 180 students each. One cluster houses K–2, while a second accommodates grades 3 and 4 and the third takes care of grades 5 and 6. Within each cluster are six classrooms accommodating 30 pupils each. The architects also layered the school's major functions into a three-part arrangement with the clusters zigzagging along one edge, common spaces such as the gym and auditorium holding down the other edge, and a multistory circulation spine running in between. Exposed ducts, pipes, and structural members—all brightly colored—add to a sense of animation and vitality. By breaking the school into a series of interconnected volumes of varying sizes and heights, the architects gave each one its own identity and avoided creating spaces that might overwhelm the children.

Occupying a broad flat site several miles outside downtown Columbus, the school presents relatively flat brick elevations on the two sides containing the common spaces. On the opposite elevations, however, HHPA expressed the classroom clusters with bold glass-and-metal compositions topped by sharply angled roofs. The result is a dramatic arrangement of forms that reflects the school's basic organization.

Note

1. Mildred Schmertz, "An Open Plan School," *Architectural Record,* September 1973, pp. 121–128.

Exposed pipes, ducts, and structural members add a sense of animation to interiors.

The school was the first in Columbus, Indiana, to employ an open plan.

Classroom modules are terraced into the hillside.

Kent Elementary School, 1972
Boston, Massachusetts

Earl R. Flansburgh & Associates, architect

90,000 square feet

700 students

Urban schools often pose unusual challenges, but this 700-pupil K–6 facility presented the added difficulty of a steeply sloping 2.7-acre site. Located in the Charlestown section of Boston, the 90,000-square-foot building uses a classroom module that matches the neighborhood's residential scale and establishes a visual rhythm similar to that of nearby nineteenth-century row houses. To help the school fit in, the architects specified a waterstruck brick that matches that of a nearby church and many other neighbors and aligned the height of

Waterstruck brick that matches a nearby church helps the school fit into its setting.

the school's main entrance with the cornice line of adjacent houses.

Making the most of the steep site, Flansburgh & Associates tucked large elements such as the gymnasium and auditorium into the hillside and stacked the classroom modules in three levels. Like many new schools of the time, Kent Elementary adopted a modified version of the open plan, grouping classrooms around a "team center." While each classroom opens onto the team center, it can be closed off completely with movable partitions. Because community use was an important element in the school's program, areas such as the gym, auditorium, library, and a community room are all accessible during after-school hours.

Skylight brings natural light into a multistory space.

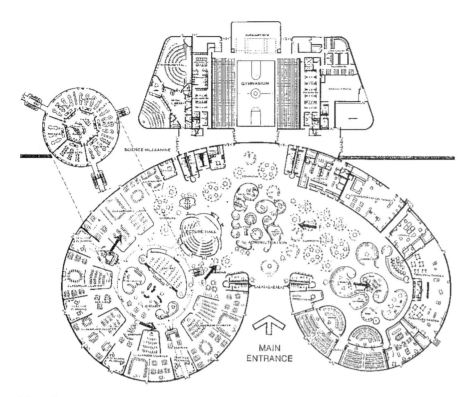

Floor plan.

Another example of architect John Shaver's attempt to break away from the traditional box, Freedom High is most commonly known as the "kidney school." With its curving walls and unorthodox plan, it certainly eliminates any danger of reminding students of other dull, prisonlike schools.

A three-building complex connected by underground tunnels, the school features a circular science center, a trapezoid-shaped gymnasium, and a kidneylike main structure. In the science center and main building, classrooms and laboratories fan out around the perimeter of each structure, while common facilities such as a library, a lecture hall, administra-

The school comprises a kidney-shaped main structure, a trapezoidal gym, and a circular science center.

tive offices, and dining area occupy the center. The 34 classrooms are organized into clusters of three or four teaching areas separated by teaching-planning and seminar spaces. While the classrooms curl around half of the main building, lecture halls for business classes and shops for various trades occupy the perimeter of the other half.

The physical education wing includes a 3000-seat central gymnasium, two practice courts, and an auxiliary gym.

The 3000-seat gymnasium can also be used for musical events.

Fodrea Community School, 1974
Columbus, Indiana
CRS (now CRSS Architects), architect
57,000 square feet
300 students (elementary school only)

Designed to provide year-round educational, vocational, and recreational facilities for the entire community, Fodrea Community School is committed to learning as a part of daily life.

Assembled with an industrialized building system, the two-story school features a space frame supported on concrete columns and an exterior skin of enamel-finished metal panels and glass. The exposed space frame running the entire length and width of the interior boldly expresses the school board's policy that adult and elementary education are (literally) under one roof. The building's open metal frame carries electrical and mechanical services, allowing a great deal of flexibility in arranging interior spaces. The key organizing element inside the school is a main concourse that encourages interaction. Within the split-level design, open-plan

Exterior skin includes enamel-finished metal panels and glass.

Main entrance.

classroom areas overlook a two-story-high media center. Stairs and ramps funnel children from the mezzanine to the media center, and a tunnel connects the learning areas with the dining room. The school's interior spaces and curving ramps embody the educators' objectives of a free exchange of information.

In its design, Fodrea Community School employed the so-called squatters approach. CRS assembled a comprehensive team of architects, engineers, and consultants on site and invited prospective users and the public to witness and participate in

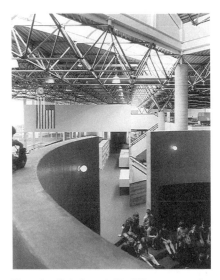
The school's industrial building system is evident on the inside.

Concrete columns support a metal space frame.

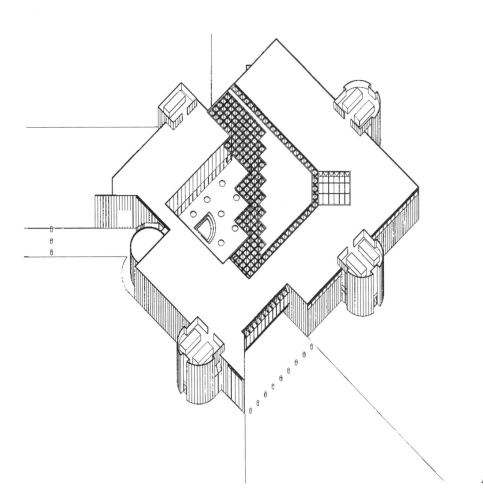
Axonometric rendering.

the school's design. Squatting in whatever spaces were available, the design teams and client worked round the clock in an initial burst of creative energy. Developed as a holistic approach to architecture, bringing all design disciplines and concerned parties together on site, the squatters process received a great deal of attention in the 1960s and 1970s. More recently, the design charrettes used by Andres Duany and Elizabeth Plater-Zyberk in planning new communities owe a certain debt to CRS' squatters.

The building's open metal frame, carrying electrical and mechanical services, allows flexibility in arranging interior spaces.

Charlestown High School and Community School, 1976
Charlestown, Massachusetts

HMFH Architects

235,000 square feet

1000 students

This urban high school was designed in the belief that a better environment produces not only better students, but ones who treat their surroundings better. When it was featured in *Architectural Record* in April 1980, architect Fenton Hollander of HMFH said,[1] "Some were not sure that there would be time for photographs," because its inner-city denizens would subject it to rapid vandalism. Today there are signs of a few problems with graffiti and general wear, but no worse than in other more affluent areas.

The Charlestown High School complex accommodates 1000 students in a six-story academic building and a two-level physical education building, connected by a bridge across a major street. Because the school is located at the edge of a blue-collar neighborhood, the architects broke down the mass of the building by carving out large recesses within its facades and projecting a series of angled light monitors above the roof. The steel-frame buildings are clad in a jumbo brick that is economical to use and easy to maintain.

Inside the school, HMFH used bright colors, light streaming down from clerestory windows, and careful manipulation of two-story spaces to create an energized environment. Because common facilities, such as an auditorium and a cafeteria, are often open to the community, they are located on the main floor. The architects organized classrooms into two wings on each of the top two floors, creating four "houses" of 250 students. Each wing has its own student lounge and can operate semiautonomously from the others.

Note

1. Charles K. Hoyt, "Working from Basics: Three Projects by Hill, Miller, Friedlander, and Hollander," *Architectural Record*, pp. 101–110.

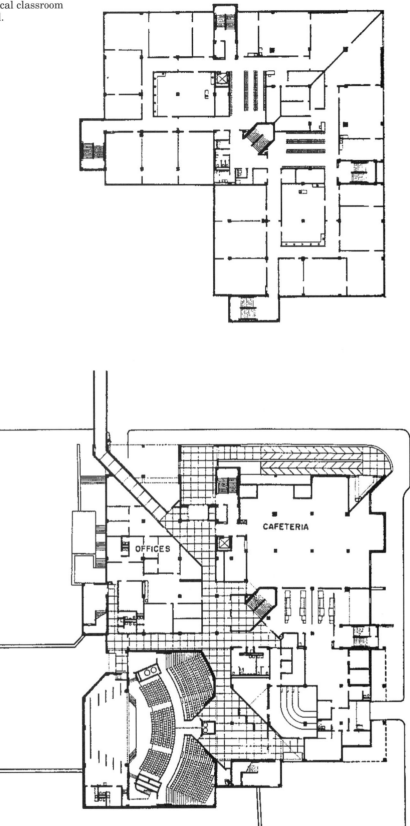

Typical classroom level.

Main floor.

The school's brick architecture helps it fit in with its blue-collar neighborhood.

The architects broke down the mass of the 6-story school by carving out large recesses and using large windows on upper floors.

Nantucket Elementary School, 1978

Nantucket, Massachusetts

Earl R. Flansburgh & Associates, architect

59,000 square feet

600 students

The design of the Nantucket Elementary School blends the many requirements of a modern school facility with responsiveness to the physical context and architectural traditions of the island. Nantucket has a distinctive architectural heritage of simple, clapboard structures and all new building on the island is governed by a local historical commission. The challenge facing Earl R. Flansburgh & Associates was to design a contemporary elementary school that would be the largest building on the island, while maintaining the character of the local architecture with its small scale, subtlety of color, and simplicity of detail.

The architects' solution was a one-story structure that retains the saltbox forms and gray clapboard siding of its older neighbors. Inside, the architects designed three teaching clusters, each with six classrooms grouped around a multipurpose activity area. Different colors help give each cluster its own identity. In the center of all the clusters sits a library, one level down from the classrooms. Special-use spaces, such as an art room, special education resource center, gym-cafeteria, and music room spread out along the other end of the school's circulation spine.

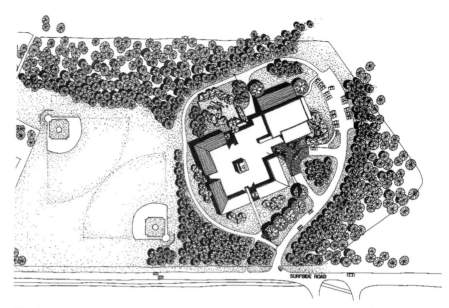

Site plan.

Classrooms are clustered around multipurpose rooms.

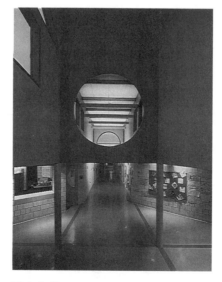

Main hallway.

Exterior view shows how the architects blended modern forms with the local tradition of saltbox architecture.

3

Current Issues in School Architecture

While school construction was sluggish during the first half of the 1980s, building activity began to pick up the middle of the decade, as the children of the post-World War II baby boomers reached school age. The picture, of course, varied from one part of the country to another, with regions such as the Southwest and West experiencing rapid growth in their school-age populations, and other areas remaining more stable. The years 1985 to 1991, which for the purposes of this book are seen as "the present," were a time of renewed interest in education. Ex-hippies and recent yuppies, who had spent the previous two decades dropping out and then cashing in, suddenly turned their attention to the need for new schools as their children reached school age. Politicians took note and at least paid lip service to the issue of education.

Although attention to a problem does not always result in a quality response, many schools built during the past six years benefited from a new climate of caring. A new generation of parents, which had grown up questioning authority, was more willing to accept nontraditional solutions to the problems of education. At the same time, architects were questioning many of Modernism's knee-jerk responses to design challenges and were trying their hand at creating buildings that respond more particularly to their surroundings and historical settings. Whether they were Postmodern or Modern or any other brand of architecture, many of the new schools fitted in better with their neighbors and were more responsive to the local climate. The best of them featured important social spaces such as courtyards, libraries, and student centers and a balanced relationship between outdoors and indoors. Their architects carefully manipulated natural light, multistory spaces, and durable materials to create lively interiors that remind students that schools can be exciting places for learning.

The projects shown in the following portfolio reflect many of the ideas mentioned above. Although they come from all parts of the country and range from totally new buildings to additions and renovations, all of the featured projects echo a common message: that the buildings in which our children go to school can be important factors in the quality of their education. All the buildings profiled in this chapter show that the people behind them—architects, educators, and government officials—cared.

Instead of making broad generalizations about the state of school architecture in the latter half of the 1980s, this chapter identifies a few of the most important issues that architects must confront when designing for education. Although not a comprehensive list of all key issues in school design, it serves as a good starting point.

Major Concerns in Designing Schools

Identity

There is only one given when designing a school: that no two projects are alike. The program for each school should reflect the client's unique needs and concerns. Understanding exactly what those needs are is no simple matter—for either the client or the architect. Through a great deal of discussion, listening, and questioning, though, architect and client should be able to put down on paper not only the physical requirements of the building but also some of the less tangible (but no less important) characteristics that will give the school its own personality.

Going to School

Architect Lawrence Perkins once wrote[1] "Seeing, approaching, entering, and becoming part of a school are not separate steps. Going toward, and going into a school are one. You see the building from a distance, then you see into the building, then you are in the building without being conscious of a defined entry." It is Perkins' philosophy that "going to school" should be a gradual, natural action and that "when we say the school is part of the world around it, the phrase is more than figurative."

Public Spaces

Successful schools not only deal with the particulars (how many classrooms, how many offices, how much storage space), but with the more general public spaces that often set the tone for the entire building.

The visitor entering practically any school in the United States is greeted by a sign stating "Visitors must report to the office." In the well-designed facility, the office is readily identifiable and easy to reach. In others, the visitor literally becomes a rat in a maze. Once located, the office can welcome or alienate the visitor. The main office should be the front door, the hub, the symbol of the school.

In recent years there has been a trend to locating the main office off a "great space" that serves as the main interior crossroad of the school. Often the cafeteria is directly related to this space as is the auditorium. The space then serves as a reception area, student commons, and lobby for performing-arts events.

The library, especially when it is also a community resource, is another element that can be designed as a memorable public space. In a few cases architects have designed the library with no walls, open to the rest of the school. But most architects still treat the library as an enclosed space, although they sometimes open it to other parts of the school by using interior windows and glazing. Enclosure not only provides acoustic privacy but security—an issue that has gained importance as the number of expensive computers and multimedia equipment used in libraries has proliferated.

Looking for a model to help shape an approach to public space that a typical student would respond positively to, many architects have turned to the shopping mall. Indeed, some architects even refer to the circulation spines in their school designs as "malls" or "educational shopping centers." A growing number of schools now use a mall-like space as the central organizing element in their plan, radiating other public spaces and classroom wings from this activity hub.

The Plan

While every plan should respond to the project's particular site, size, climate, and programmatic demands, schools tend to fall naturally into one of several different plan types. The reason for this is simple: The basic elements of every school (classrooms, public spaces, circulation spine, administration offices, recreational facilities, etc.) tend to remain the same and the relationships between these elements do not vary greatly. For example, shared facilities such as libraries and cafeterias are usually placed in a central location to provide equal access from all parts of the school. Similarly, gymnasiums make the most sense when located adjacent to outdoor playfields. Educational fads certainly affect the way schools are laid out, but certain basic floor plans (or variations thereof) surface over and over.

The Compact Plan. For many years the most common of all layouts, the compact plan is still the approach most often selected for urban schools. Because it minimizes the amount of land, perimeter-wall area, and interior circulation space needed, this two- or three-story plan can be cost-effective. To relieve the monotony of a closed interior, architects sometimes arrange the plan around a central courtyard. Adding to schools designed with compact plans, though, can be a problem because they usually are self-contained structures that turn in on either a central courtyard or some other kind of interior space.

The Loft Plan. First made possible by air conditioning, this plan adapts an industrial approach made popular by old loft buildings. Large expanses of easily divisible space, often lit from skylights above, are a hallmark of this plan and allow for great economy and flexibility. In the 1960s and 1970s educators and architects realized the loft-plan school was easy to convert to the then-popular open plan. The building-systems approach to school design also lent itself naturally to the loft plan. An early loft-plan school was the Hillsdale High School in San Mateo, California (see p. 36). Another was the 250,000-square-foot Linton High School in Schenectady, New York (Perkins & Will, 1958). Describing that school, the architects stated that it will probably remind visitors more of a contemporary industrial or commercial complex than of the traditional multistory school it replaced.

The Finger Plan. A simple arrangement in which classrooms spread out from a central corridor, the finger plan can be easily expanded by merely continuing the circulation spine and adding more fingers. Because it provides all classrooms with direct access to the outside and allows natural ventilation, this plan is still a popular solution in areas with temperate climates.

The Campus Plan. A series of individual buildings arranged on a site, the campus plan can help break down the massing and scale of a large institution. Modeled after colleges and college-preparatory schools, the plan usually can be easily expanded by just adding another individual building. The buildings can define quads and other outdoor spaces that can be used as important shared amenities. The campus plan, though, may not make much sense in harsh climates where inclement weather makes walking between buildings undesirable.

The Cluster Plan. A variation of the campus plan, this arrangement can be described as a collection of small schoolhouses linked by enclosed hallways. The enclosed connections eliminate the problems caused in harsh climates by the campus plan. Like the campus plan, this approach offers easy expansion possibilities. It can also reflect the organization of a school by subject, grade level, or "houses."

Classroom Size

The questions that educational consultants most often hear concern the size of educational spaces. Although good consultants usually explain that a particular project's program should determine the size of various facilities, administrators and architects always want justification for the dimensions of their proposed rooms or a benchmark they can use in comparing their facilities with those of some national "average." "Average" or "minimum," however, all too often become the standard. As a result, they should be resisted by architects and clients alike.

With that caveat stated, let me just briefly touch on the subject of classroom size. Please note that all sizes are given as ranges, not absolutes. You can't go wrong, though, if you err on the side of more space.

Classroom Size by Grade

Grade	Area SF	Area per child in largest class, SF
K	1000–1200	40–50
1–3	750–900	25–30
4–6	750–900	25–30
7–12	575–750	20–25

Space standards need to be developed with care. A famous example comes from California. When state funding of school construction was mandated, a panel of educators and architects was charged with the task of developing standards. They recommended 110 square feet per pupil for elementary schools, a figure consistent with prevailing norms. The legislature then cut the figure to 55 square feet because they reasoned educators and architects always ask for twice as much as they need.

The trend to standardize space requirements is, in part, a reaction to court decisions mandating more equality in school facilities. How this complicated issue is resolved will influence future school design. It would be unfortunate, though, if court mandates negate the need to let program influence design.

Indoor–Outdoor Relationships

Most architects today understand the importance of bringing natural light and views into school interiors and relating appropriate rooms to outdoor spaces. Many of the schools profiled in this chapter make special efforts to weave indoors and outdoors together, using such elements as courtyards, plazas, light wells, and extensive glazing to reinforce this relationship. The days of the hermetically sealed institution, isolated from its surroundings are over. Even in urban settings, architects are carving out small plazas and bringing more sunlight inside.

While athletics is perhaps the most obvious program requiring access to outdoor facilities, it is not the only one. Classrooms, especially those designed for younger students as well as art and science programs, can all benefit from access to outdoor areas. An increasingly popular program at many schools is child care; as with kindergartens, access to the outdoors is essential for these small children.

A school's site itself can also be a teaching tool. In Williamsburg, Virginia, a high school is related to an adjacent nature park, complete with a swamp where students from all parts of the district come for environmental education. Students use the park to relate their science curriculum to actual situations. They can even catch their own frogs in the swamp for you know what. In Palacios, Texas, the school district maintains a marine-biology center for its own students and those from surrounding communities.

Establishing Character

What should a school building look like? Think for a minute about your image of a school. If you grew up in the 1920s and 1930s, your school was probably one of the most imposing buildings in town. The building was generally two or three stories high with an imposing exterior designed in anything from Gothic to Spanish Colonial or Greek Revival. Inside, the school was essentially a series of one-room cells stacked on top of each other. It seems as though there must have been a Johnny Appleseed traveling the country with one floor plan and applying whatever face was in vogue with the local school board at the time.

In the 1940s and 1950s the basic plan remained essentially the same, but most of the building's decorative details were lost. Then in the 1960s the Modern glass box became the most common model. Today school architects are more sensitive to the unique character of each area in which they work. The result has been a growing trend toward regionalism in design. The Capital High School in Santa Fe, New Mexico (p. 95), for example, is a conscious effort to reflect the state's Territorial style of architecture with its columned entrance and courtyards. In contrast, Sunderland Elementary School (p. 91) in Massachusetts is an obvious response to New England's heritage of clapboard buildings.

This same concern is also expressed in school interiors. Architect Wilmont Vickrey says that where appropriate his firm incorporates ethnic or community-based design elements to help children feel at ease. For example, he points to the atrium corridor of a Chicago school designed by his firm that simulates a Central or South American marketplace—a reference to the school's predominantly Hispanic student body.

Community Use

Almost every new school today must accommodate community use of at least some of its facilities. Such accommodation may range from lighting all play-fields for adult use at night to opening up entire school floors for adult education and community meetings. But it is a fact of life in almost every school district in the country. And as the current wave of school-age children go on to college and as the country's population continues to age, the trend toward community use of elementary and secondary school facilities will only intensify. Indeed, without community use, many schools now being built would become unnecessary by the first decade of the twenty-first century.

The design implications of community use are many and varied. First, architects must zone schools to permit different parts of the building to be used at various times. Most community use occurs in the evening and involves major public spaces such as libraries, auditoriums, and gymnasiums. As a result, these facilities should be located close to the main entrance and must be able to operate while the rest of the school is closed. Security is a related issue that must be addressed while an architect zones a building for daytime and nighttime use. Such concerns can even affect the design of locker rooms; while the toilet facilities here may be open for adults at night, showers and lockers may best be closed to prevent theft and vandalism.

With nighttime use becoming the norm, the community as a whole (and not just parents and educators) are becoming increasingly involved in the school planning process. While this certainly makes the design and approvals process more complex, input from all future users of the building is essential.

Size

Two opposing trends are currently at work influencing school design and planning. On one hand, community use and more specialized facilities for arts education, sciences, and special education are forcing schools to get bigger and bigger. Simply put, schools are getting bigger today because more takes place there. Increasingly seen as community resources, schools must now accommodate night classes, community meetings, senior-citizen groups, and year-round athletic events. But at the same time, parents and educators are demanding smaller schools with more individualized learning environments.

One design solution to this problem of competing forces is to create "schools within a school" or "houses" that help break down a large institution into smaller entities, each with its own identity and personality. A high school of 2000 students, for example, can be organized into either four schools of 500 students each or by grade level, say, grades 9 and 10 and grades 11 and 12, each with 1000 students and its own administration.

The question of size is not a serious one in a rural community, but is a growing concern in large suburban and urban areas. In New York City, community groups are asking that middle and junior high schools be organized around groups of no more than 500 students. Both empirical data and common sense are behind this movement. Recent studies indicate that educational achievement is directly related to school and class size. The data seems to show that students learn better in small schools and small classes. At the same time, educators have long known that the bigger the school the more chance a child has to be "lost."

Human Scale

Size and scale are intimately related. And nowhere are they more important than at the early-childhood and elementary levels. One example of a school designed with children in mind is the Early Learning Center in Stamford, Connecticut. Everything here is just the right height for youngsters. The open shelving, made of boards laid on concrete blocks are just right for display, or as a work surface, or for standing on. They are low enough that, if used for standing on, falling off is not a serious risk. When asked whether adults were not uncomfortable in this environment, the school's director replied that she sincerely hoped so.

As children grow up, scale continues to be important—in both interior and outdoor spaces. The large parade ground at the Air Force Academy, for example, is perfect for a battalion of cadets, but such an anonymous space probably is not appropriate for a junior or senior high school. We must also remember that great spaces are fine for certain kinds of assembly or circulation, but schools need other places where students can be alone, have a quiet one-on-one conversation, or meet in small groups.

A few years ago, this author attended a meeting at Cranbrook Academy in Michigan. This author, on returning to the school late one evening, took a stroll around the grounds. The experience at night is different from that during the day. The columns at the art museum-library entrance take on an entirely different feeling. At the end of the library the author discovered a wall detail, which prompted him to walk down a narrow passage to get a different view of a statue of Europa. The narrow passage ended at a small balcony area. On arriving, the author discovered a young man sitting on a bench, enjoying a quiet moment of contemplation. So the author walked toward the Orpheus fountain and found a young man and woman with their arms around each other, oblivious to the author's presence. As the author walked toward Lake Jonah, he heard several voices and the laughter of children. Further investigation revealed a young family playing what can only be described as a game of flashlight hide-and-seek on the meadow behind a dorm. This at 11 o'clock at night!

That evening walk around Cranbrook revealed to this author more of the genius of Eliel Saarinen, the school's designer and president from 1932 to 1942, than 1000 photographs of the place ever could. The buildings and grounds of Cranbrook underscore Saarinen's deep understanding of scale, materials, and the relationship between indoor and outdoor spaces.

Energy Concerns

In all parts of the country, education-facility managers are again attending seminars and workshops on energy conservation. The increased activity recalls the concerns of the educational community following the 1972–1973 oil embargo. Interestingly, many school districts that had adopted energy policies in the 1970s found themselves in the 1980s sliding back to their wasteful preembargo ways.

To reduce energy consumption school boards are putting together sophisticated energy-management plans that outline the responsibilities of all concerned parties, from superintendent all the way down to principals, teachers, and maintenance workers. Many of these plans include installation of state-of-the-art environmental-control systems that regulate buildings' use of heating, air conditioning, and lighting.

According to a recent study conducted by the American Association of School Administrators, the nation's schools spent $7.4 billion for energy in 1991–1992, up $490 million from the year before. The same study stated that effective energy management could save the country's schools $1.85 billion a year. Unfortunately, many schools are unable to pay for the repairs and control systems that would save them money in the long run.

In addition, architects are reexamining low-tech(nology) approaches to energy conservation that include proper orientation to winter sun, shading from direct summer sun, natural lighting to reduce artificial light use, and natural ventilation.

Designing for Technology

Today's youngsters are becoming computer literate in the very early grades. Schools without some kind of a computer capability are now the exception, rather than the rule. Many states now mandate computer literacy as a requirement for grade promotion or graduation.

When computers first became a presence in schools, educators put them in special rooms as if they could be taught as a distinct subject, separate from the rest of the curriculum. Today computers have moved into the classroom and are treated as tools for teaching any subject. Looking to the future, some observers predict every student will soon have his or her own electronic notebook that will serve as calculator, personal library, writing pad, and video-display terminal. When the student goes home, the electronic notebook and all its capabilities go along. If the student can't come to school one day, he or she can connect electronically. Unfortunately for many a delinquent student, "the dog ate my homework" excuse will have lost its last shred of plausibility. The new excuse may have to involve a computer virus zapping a child's hard work.

The impact of computers is being felt beyond the classroom, too. Computer-controlled energy-management systems are helping to save money by making schools more efficient users of heating, air conditioning, and electricity. Computers are also being used to compose and play music, control lights and curtains in school plays, and send messages to students. Some people predict that chalkboards, overhead projectors, large TV sets, and other "traditional" teaching tools will soon be replaced by electronic screens displaying text and related visual aids. The immediate problem facing architects is wiring schools so computer terminals can be located wherever they might be needed. Although few schools have gone to the expense of installing raised flooring with wiring underneath everywhere, such a solution may be common in the not-too-distant future.

Designs That Accommodate Expansion

The mobility of Americans today makes planning school facilities extremely difficult. Changes in the economic strength of one state or another can set off new waves of migration. Many of the families who moved to Texas during its oil boom in the 1970s, for example, picked up stakes again in the 1980s and set out for greener pastures. In-migration has become so extreme in California, for instance, that 30 percent of state-financed school construction must be relocatable units. Designing attractive schools with both permanent and relocatable spaces is a major challenge to architects in the state. In other states without such requirements, many school boards are asking architects to at least consider during the initial design stage how schools might be expanded later on.

Although there are many different ways of adding onto an existing school, most fall into one of the following general types:

- A perimeter or wraparound addition that includes modernization of the existing building plus construction of one or more additions closely connected to the perimeter of the old facility.

- Short-link additions that are attached to the existing building by a short connecting segment.

- Long-link additions that are nearly free-standing structures, connected to the existing building by a long, narrow, enclosed or open segment.

- Plug-in additions inserted into an existing building where its structure or floor plan makes it possible.

- Stack-on additions in which one or more stories are added to the existing building. This approach is seldom used in the school field.

- Captured space in which an outdoor court in the center of a school or between two wings is roofed over.

Additions sometimes do more than just offer extra square footage. In a few examples show in this portfolio, new construction has totally transformed a school, giving it a new personality throughout. (See the Mount Carmel Elementary School on p. 148, Penn High School on p. 91, and Berkley Community School on p. 98.) Additions can also reorient a building, turning the front, for example, away from a busy, noisy street and moving the main entrance to a less dangerous road.

Note

1. Lawrence Perkins, *Work Place for Learning,* Reinhold Publishing Corporation, New York, 1957, p. 8.

Portfolio of Recent Projects

The projects presented in the following portfolio reflect many of the design consideration mentioned in this chapter. Although they are only a small sampling of the work being done throughout the country, they represent some of the best schools being designed today.

Charles Haskell Elementary School, 1985
Edmund, Oklahoma
HTB Architects
41,200 square feet

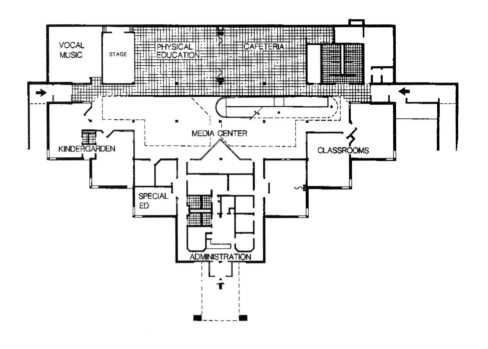

Dug into the crown of a hill to protect itself from the often harsh prairie elements, this 41,200-square-foot school makes the most of its site. Earth-sheltered on its north face, the school uses passive solar energy to stay warm in the winter and a simple exhaust system to keep cool in the summer. The key ingredient in this solar-energy system is a double-skin roof that traps warm air. In the winter the air is circulated throughout the building, while in the summer it is expelled by fans through vents in the roof.

The school's most dramatic feature is the multistory media center that occupies its core and is fully wired for computers and video systems. A curving ramp and upper-story bridges inject a healthy dose of motion to the room, while the school's plan surrounds the space with classrooms. Realizing the need to separate younger pupils from older ones, HTB Architects placed kindergarten rooms along one edge of the media center and arranged the

West facade.

The media center.

other classrooms on either the opposite edge or the upper floor. At the intersection of the two main corridors, the architects placed administration offices and special education rooms.

To encourage team teaching and offer greater flexibility in educational approaches, the architects designed the 800-square-foot classrooms in clusters of four and equipped them with movable walls. Whenever large groups must be accommodated, teachers can move walls out of the way and create any combination of two, three, or four rooms.

The school currently handles 450 students, but was designed so that it could be expanded. The building's site on 25 acres also provides enough room for the future construction of a middle school and the creation of an educational campus.

East facade.

Stow-Munroe Falls High School, 1987
Stow, Ohio

Richard Fleischman Architects

254,800 square feet

This school was called "Stow's new gentle giant" by one observer, who wrote,[1] "Stripped down to the bare essentials, it looks like a no-nonsense workplace for a large number of students to pursue a basic modern education." With 254,800 square feet, the school can accommodate 1800 students.

Architect Richard Fleischman sees the new school as "an encyclopedia of learning." He calls the central hall "the corridor of action" and says the bridgelike section of the space reminds him of the Ponte Vecchio in Florence. According to Fleischman, the main portal is a gateway comparable to the Statue of Liberty, the Eiffel Tower, or St. Louis' Gateway Arch.

Fleischman likes to describe his projects and leave it to the viewer to respond. "The bridge serves as a boulevard and it accommodates many activities during the school day, evening hours, and weekends. Users can constantly be exposed to a variety of educational opportunities and are encouraged to participate."

"It is essential that the two learning centers—library and cafeteria/great hall—are strategically located on the east-west and north-south axes. The curriculum is designed to direct the learners to avail themselves of the respective resource centers." The "cafeteria/great hall," a focal point on the school's boulevard, helps span the customary gap between the classroom and the more active areas of the school.

Note

1. Wilma Salisbury, "Stow's New Gentle Giant," *Cleveland Plain Dealer* magazine, July 19, 1987, pp. 20–21.

Entry portals give the school a civic presence.

Natural light and two-story spaces animate interiors.

The school has been called the town's "gentle giant."

Desert View Elementary School, 1988
Sunland Park, New Mexico

Perkins & Will with Mimbres, associated architects

43,800 square feet

The Desert View Elementary School program called for a 43,800-square-foot school for 600 students. Architects Perkins & Will responded with a budget-conscious, prototype school that translates simple concrete block and bar joists into eye-catching structures for about $50 per square foot.

The 25-acre site features an arid, desert landscape adjacent to a residential area populated by recent arrivals from Texas and Mexico. The school is intended to bring order to a highly fragmented residential area, bordered on one side by a highway and the Rio Grande and on the other side by the Santa Fe Railroad, the border of Mexico, and mountains. A public plaza and the main facade of the school face the community. This plan helps define the termination of the neighborhood and gives the school an urban presence befitting its social role.

A decision was made early on to keep the school small in scale. Instead of one big, campuslike elementary school to accommodate the town's entire student population, three identical facilities were built about ¼ mile apart—one each for grades K–2, 3–4, and 5–6. Compatible age groupings were one object of the scheme. Another was taking advantage of limited land parcels readily available on the periphery of the community.

Two ideas influenced the architectural composition of the complex. One was to make a clear delineation of the natural from the manufactured. This was accomplished by surrounding the school and irrigated portions of the site with a circular rock wall. Outside, the landscape remains unchanged. The second was to allude to the area's vernacular architecture without directly imitating it. The school's sloped metal roofs, pastel-colored masonry walls,

Canvas awnings help shade an outdoor walkway.

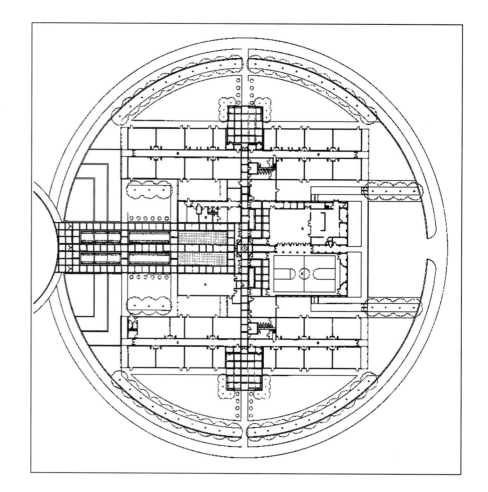

The architects carefully integrated out-door areas with indoor spaces.

The main corridor serves as an indoor street.

Although modest in size, the school offers an imposing front elevation.

and decorative wrought-iron railing recall the unassuming, practical architecture of the area. The metal farm sheds of the region are also recalled in the design of the school's entry tower and entry-court portal.

The plan is organized into three essential functional subtypes: the classrooms, which are repetitive units; the library and administrative areas; and the multipurpose pavilion and cafeteria, which are shared by the school and the community. The entry tower, the cafeteria, and the multipurpose pavilion are dominant formal elements and symbolize the school's importance to the community. Materials for the project include a dramatic combination of natural and synthetic elements such as rocks, glazed-concrete masonry units, standing-seam metal roofs, exposed painted structural steel, and translucent fiberglass roof canopies and canvas awnings.

The varied fenestration—ranging from tiny windows to entire gable ends—helps give the building a much larger, grander sense of scale than its relatively modest size would ordinarily evoke. Similarly, integral color in the concrete-block-bearing walls and the bright paint of the exposed steel structure give a festive elegance to the forthright materials.

The school blends regional forms with a modern vocabulary.

Gatzert Elementary School, 1988
Seattle, Washington

Burr Lawrence Rising & Bates
Architects

52,600 square feet

Like many urban schools, Gatzert
Elementary is located on a small
site, in this case a 6-acre parcel in
Seattle's diversified international
district. With a heavily trafficked
street to the north and commercial
and residential buildings on both the
north and the south, the school was
built as a much-needed oasis in a
tight urban fabric.

   A child care center with its own
entrance is incorporated in the building. Privately operated, it is open to
all children in the community, providing before- and after-school care
as well as all-day care. The kinder-
garten/day-care outdoor play spaces
are enclosed by masonry walls and

View of north facade.

welded vertical-steel fencing to allow for visual control, while creating safe outdoor play spaces.

The school's central hub is the commons, which also serves as a dining facility. This architecturally dramatic space is located directly off the main student entrance. Adjacent to the hub is the gymnasium, separated from the commons by an acoustical folding wall. When needed, the folding wall can be opened so that the gymnasium, commons, and stage can function as one large, flexible community gathering space. The learning resource center also borders the commons and is accessible for community use because of its central location. Students walk by and encounter this space many times during the day. Also located directly off the commons is the kitchen, with the central administration area conveniently nearby.

Classrooms are located at the perimeter of the building to maximize daylight in all educational spaces. Natural light is introduced into the interior core area—the learning resource center, an art-science room, and support spaces—from overhead by the use of skylights and clerestories.

To create a strong, inviting entry the architects combined shed roofs, a colonnade, angular brick walls, and translucent roof panels. Sloped roofs offer a low scale for small children and reduce the impact of large-scale elements located in the interior core of the facility. The materials and scale of the school are pleasantly compatible with the surrounding urban setting.

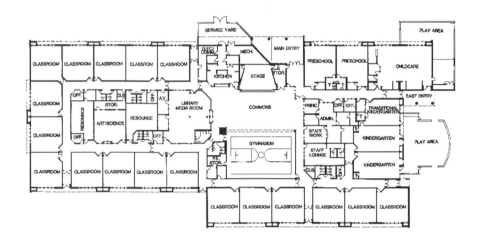

The commons is the school's central hub.

Sunderland Elementary School, 1989
Sunderland, Massachusetts

Earl R. Flansburgh & Associates,
architects

41,500 square feet

Located in a rural town in the Connecticut River valley of western Massachusetts, this one-story school doubles as an important civic center. Because the building had to accommodate town meetings and community gatherings, as well as all of the usual school functions, Earl R. Flansburgh & Associates gave it a prominent civic profile with an open metal bell tower at its heart. Inside the building, the architects organized classrooms and public spaces along two intersecting corridors, as if they were streets and the school were a microcosm of a rural town.

The metal-stud structure is clad in clapboard and cedar shingles, so it fits in with other buildings in this fertile tobacco-growing area. The architects also echo regional building forms in the school's barn-like library and the storytelling "silo" attached to it.

Bell tower.

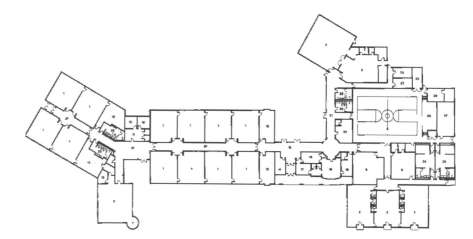

Aware that the school's youngest pupils should be put at ease, Flansburgh designed the kindergarten wing as a set of three gable-roofed houses and brought it to the front of the building. The use of residential forms, coupled with the kindergarten's orientation to the sun-drenched south, gives this part of the school the warm feeling of home. The rest of the school recalls the informal clustering of farm buildings so often found in this part of the state.

Storytelling silo.

Dining room.

The school's architecture recalls the informal clustering of farm buildings.

A new entry.

New facilities and wings envelop an older building.

Penn High School, 1989
Osceola, Indiana

Greiner (formerly Daverman)
HMFH, associated architects

460,000 square feet

Billed as "a high school for the 21st century," Penn High School combines good design with an elaborate program and the latest technological gadgets. Although it's hard to tell today, the school began as a nondescript 1950s building. Three years of phased expansion and renovation, though, transformed the outdated structure into essentially a new complex. New facilities—including a performing-arts pavilion, a physical-fitness area, and a practical arts and vocational education wing—envelop the old building. In addition, the school received an entirely new main entrance that provides a grander introduction to the new institution.

Instead of designing the new facilities as individual additions, the architects tried to piece them together so that they would appear as a single new complex. Rather than highlighting differences in materials and colors, the architects blurred distinctions between old and new. At the same time, they clustered educational components so that related disciplines (such as math and science or English and performing arts) would be grouped together. While there is a cohesiveness to the entire design, each of these educational components has its own identity and character. Without such divisions the 460,000-square-foot school might very well have been overwhelming in scale.

At the heart of the school is the library or "instructional materials center," around which spin the major academic departments. Penn High School's high-tech library features a computer voice-data video interface that hooks up to other libraries, information networks, data exchanges, and even the Library of Congress.

Because they must be able to operate independently of the rest of the school and be open after school hours, the physical education area and the performing-arts center both have their own dramatic entrance lobbies. During the school day, however, these components are fully integrated with the rest of the institution.

Helping Penn live up to its billing as a school of the future are programs in such fields as robotics, laser technologies, fiber optics, genetics, and plastics. In addition, a fully integrated telecommunications system utilizing voice-video and data via fiber optics connects every classroom to on-site research facilities (such as the library) and can provide satellite linkage to information sources throughout the country.

A new day-care center adjacent to the practical arts and vocational education wing offers hands-on experience to students interested in child development and provides child-care services for faculty and the community. To help the small children feel more comfortable, the architects gave the day-care center a residential character.

The library or "instructional materials center."

The physical education wing has its own lobby and entrance.

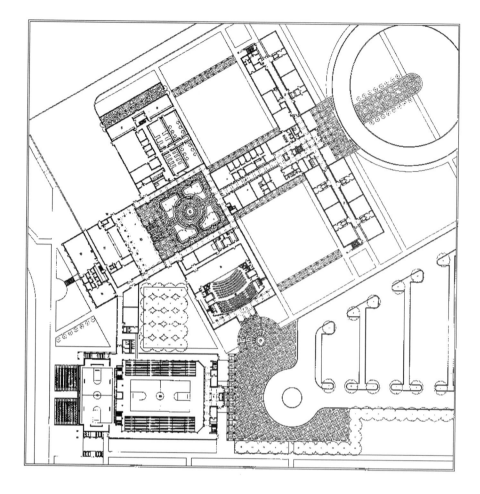

This 800-student high school (planned for expansion to a capacity of 1300 pupils) is located at the southern edge of a growing residential area in Santa Fe, New Mexico. The 45-acre site is characterized by a desert landscape and is crossed by an arroyo, or drainage swale, which serves as a green belt for the expanding community of single-family homes to the south.

The architects planned the school as a series of interconnected symmetrical pavilion blocks, oriented in response to the site and the surrounding vistas. Two parallel rows of pavilions—one the main classroom block and the other for arts and sciences—line up along the arroyo and look toward the mountain views to the northeast. Crossing these blocks and connecting them is the more formal and public spine of the school, which includes administration offices, dining hall, and a landscaped courtyard. The gymnasium pavilion is split off from the rest of the school and helps define yet another courtyard.

View of model.

The school's architectural language derives from the combination of adobe and neoclassical forms found in the Territorial style. Composed of arcades, towers, plazas, courtyards, and decorative brick cornices, the Territorial style is often used on public buildings in New Mexico. At Capital High the architects used towers to define the two main entrances: the first anchors a circular bus-loading plaza and marks the student entrance, while the second marks the public entrance. Inside the school, natural light floods the two-story circulation spine and other important spaces from clerestory windows.

By employing the Territorial style and materials native to the Southwest, Perkins & Will gave Capital High School the look and character of an important public building, while fostering pride in the region's heritage.

Towers and arcades mark the main entrances.

The library.

A courtyard.

The architects applied the vocabulary of the Territorial style to a modern building.

Deerwood Elementary School, 1989
Egan, Minnesota

Hammel Green and Abrahamson,
architect

78,000 square feet

This is an outstanding school that has been recognized both regionally and nationally for its careful response to program. Three components combine to make Deerwood Elementary's program unusual. First, it is an elementary school for preschool through fifth grade. Second, the school houses a program for emotionally and behaviorally disturbed children. These students begin in a special preschool program as early as age three. If possible, they are mainstreamed into regular classrooms. If not, they remain in the special program throughout their school years. Finally, Deerwood School serves as a community education center. Adult-education classes, neighborhood meetings, and special community events take place here. In fact, the building tends to be as busy on evenings and weekends as it is during school hours.

Hammel Green and Abrahamson's design response was a two-story building set into its hillside site to minimize the impact of the school's 78,000 square feet on the adjacent middle-class neighborhood. Horizontal bands of chamfered brick further reduce the visual height of the building and stress the relationship with surrounding fields. In addition, the bay windows in the classrooms create a residential scale both inside and outside.

Forms express the separate functions going on within the building. The classrooms, cafeteria-gym, and instructional materials center (IMC), for example, are each announced as individual blocks on the building's exterior. At the same time, the interior of the school focuses on the large, central IMC.

Separate functions are expressed as their own blocks on the school's exterior. The cafeteria-gym block, for example, is set off from the rest of the school in the photo above.

The school fits comfortably on its site.

Here the emphasis is on creating a child-scaled environment; this is especially obvious in the reading nooks beneath the double stairway leading into the IMC. Classrooms are located around the perimeter of the IMC, with each one having an open "fourth wall." This program of open or semiopen classrooms has been the policy of this school district for over 20 years. The current configuration of three full walls, finished with veneer plaster and painted masonry, allows maximum privacy and concentration, without losing the benefits of team teaching and student interaction.

INTERMEDIATE AND LOWER LEVELS

Reading nook below stairway.

Tall windows break scale of exterior walls.

Berkley Community School, Addition and Renovation, 1989
Berkley, Massachusetts

Earl R. Flansburgh & Associates, architect

75,000 square feet (total),
54,000 square feet (new)

Starting with a flat-roofed, red-brick school that seemed to have the word "generic" stamped all over it, Earl R. Flansburgh & Associates created a lively new complex of buildings organized around an outdoor courtyard. While the architects might have continued the red-brick architecture of the original school on their addition or hidden it behind a new facade or building, they incorporated it into their design, so it rests like a comfortable old shirt in a fashionable new outfit.

Dressed with split-faced concrete block, the new steel-frame building offers a pleasing contrast to the older brick structure. The school's plan, though, flows directly from the old building's, attaching itself fully to the original layout. Together the old and the new structures define a new central courtyard that brings daylight into the school

The recent additions blend easily with the existing school (far right in photo).

A new kindergarten (left in photo) gets its own circular play yard.

The library.

and provides a convenient outdoor room for gatherings and events. To give the kindergarten its own identity, the architects housed it in a separate gabled building attached at one corner to the rest of the school and designed a small curving playground for it out front. A new covered arcade extending from one end of the old building serves as a pickup-and-dropoff stand for children waiting for transportation.

Anchoring the entire new facility is a circular tower that serves as part of the school's library. Although inexpensive materials such as concrete block and gypboard predominate in the school's interiors, the architects' use of bold colors and large punched-out forms give corridors and major spaces a sense of animation.

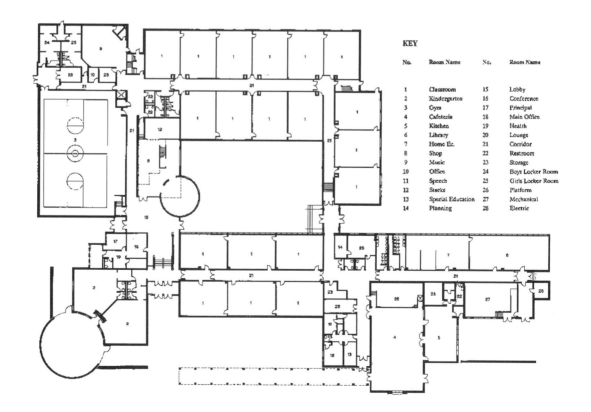

KEY

No.	Room Name	No.	Room Name
1	Classroom	15	Lobby
2	Kindergarten	16	Conference
3	Gym	17	Principal
4	Cafeteria	18	Main Office
5	Kitchen	19	Health
6	Library	20	Lounge
7	Home Ec.	21	Corridor
8	Shop	22	Restroom
9	Music	23	Storage
10	Office	24	Boys Locker Room
11	Speech	25	Girls Locker Room
12	Stacks	26	Platform
13	Special Education	27	Mechanical
14	Planning	28	Electric

Inexpensive materials such as gypboard are enlivened by bold colors and cutouts.

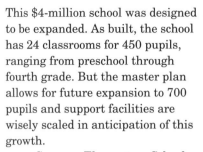

Symmes Elementary School, 1989
Cincinnati, Ohio

Baxter Hodell Donnelly Preston,
architect

53,400 square feet

This $4-million school was designed
to be expanded. As built, the school
has 24 classrooms for 450 pupils,
ranging from preschool through
fourth grade. But the master plan
allows for future expansion to 700
pupils and support facilities are
wisely scaled in anticipation of this
growth.

Symmes Elementary School
was conceived as a "home away from
home" for its young occupants. One
way the architects achieved that was
by reducing the apparent scale of the
one-story building, allowing it to quietly coexist with the surrounding single-family residential neighborhood.
Gabled roofs, windows sized and
placed for the small student, and
strong masonry treatment add to the
residential scale and feel of the
building.

Main entry facade.

Dividing the school into wings with a strong central corridor also provides smaller spaces that are not overwhelming to the student, while at the same time allowing the children to feel they are part of a larger community. Kindergarten is in one wing, lower grades in another, and upper grades in the third wing. A fourth wing is planned for the expansion. All the wings relate to a central axis or corridor that houses the general activities of the media center, art and music, physical education, cafeteria, and administrative offices. This axis also helps separate the noisier functions of physical education, music, and dining from the more quiet atmosphere of the classrooms. The media center is featured as the central element. This is to remind students of the importance of the space and encourage them to use it.

The design incorporates an interesting energy feature: Exhaust ventilators are located at the ends of the corridors to ventilate the rooms on mild days. A modular organization of mechanical and lighting systems simplifies possible changes, while natural light is also introduced into the interior through skylights placed at intersections of the main corridor and the wings.

The media center.

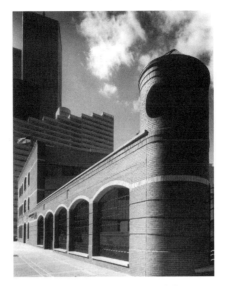

Arches and towers provide playful touches.

The school wraps around a front court-yard.

P.S. 234, 1989
New York City

Richard Dattner, architect

75,000 square feet

685 students

Dealing with the many bureaucratic demands of the New York City Board of Education might discourage an architect intent on doing good work. But it didn't deter Richard Dattner. Not only does his design for P.S. 234 suit the neighborhood where it was built and meet high aesthetic standards, but Dattner built the $14.5-million school in record time—less than 4 years, as compared with the usual 8 to 12. The project has won raves from its sharpest critics—the 685 K–5 students who go to school there.

Although Dattner did have to stick closely to the New York City Board of Education's rigorously detailed program, often down to the square inch, he was able to set up a dialog with the board's staff architects. By being able "to steal a little from this and a little from that," Dattner designed a number of unusual, informal alcoves so that the corridors become gathering places that encourage a sense of community in the school. In fact, the ground-floor entrance hall, simply called the "community area," has built-in wooden benches. Curved wooden platforms are built in on the second and third floors so that students can enjoy views of the Hudson River from a series of varied windows, including an oculus.

Although the school board's requirements for maintenance and safety dictated the materials Dattner could use, he selected a pale, neutral palette. Although he chose to create an orderly series of traditional, rectangular classrooms, in keeping with the current "back to basics" philosophy, he didn't line them up. Instead, he created distinctive entrances for each room by introducing slight chamfers and jogs along the corridors. Also of visual interest are large windows at child's eye level, high ceilings, and exposed or exaggerated structural elements. Thus Dattner was able to meet the school board's demand for no-nonsense organization and the student's need for an engaging, personalized environment.

Outside, Dattner was equally successful. Filling nearly half of a small city block in lower Manhattan's Tribeca area, the three-story school provides 75,000 square feet of educational space. The entrance of the school is demarcated by a series of red-brick piers and arches, connected by decorated steel gates designed by artist and neighborhood resident Donna Dennis. These elements

Typical classroom.

An engaged tower turns the corner.

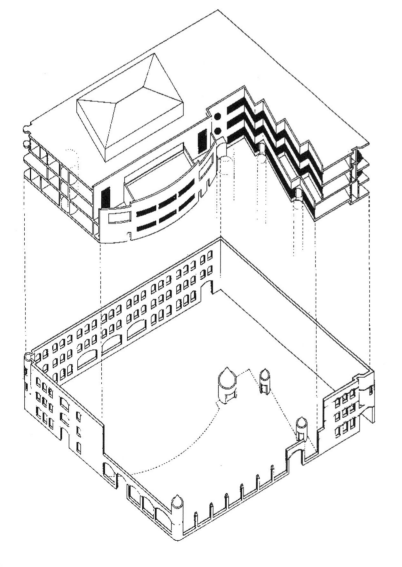

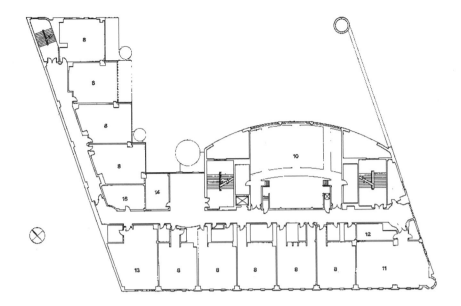

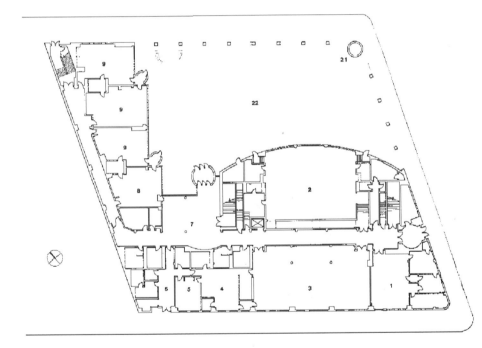

enclose a courtyard-play area that has been raised above street level to give the students a sense of privacy and protection. Four sentrylike box towers, one of which has a bell the children can ring, also convey a sense of ownership and security. In fact, the interplay between the whimsical maritime ironwork and the decorative towers conveys a sense of adventure and makes the school a thoroughly accessible, inviting environment.

The school is successfully linked to the surrounding neighborhood—mostly low-scale nineteenth-century industrial buildings—by its use of red brick. At the same time Dattner enlivened the facade with pale belt courses and narrow arched windows along the three outer walls. A sawtoothed facade formed with strip windows faces the inner courtyard. The design is so successfully integrated into the neighborhood that numerous local residents have complimented Dattner for his sensitive renovation of what they assumed was an older structure.

Jane S. Roberts Elementary
School, 1990
Dade County, Florida

Hervin Romney, architect

79,000 square feet

With its pink and turquoise roofs, its striking elevator tower, and its occasionally shifted grid, the Jane S. Roberts Elementary School seems to be one of a kind. But if the Dade County, Florida, school system follows through with its original plans, the building will be a prototype for schools in the area, a playful "kit of parts" spawning variations on a tropical theme.

Designed by Hervin Romney, a cofounder of the firm Arquitectonica who set out on his own in 1985, the school combines inexpensive materials and simple construction with a refreshing sense of whimsy. Romney kept the local climate in mind throughout the design process. As a result, most corridors and stairways are covered but not enclosed, and all classrooms look onto outdoor courtyards.

The plan of the 79,000-square-foot school is composed of four major elements—an administration block, a classroom quadrangle, a service

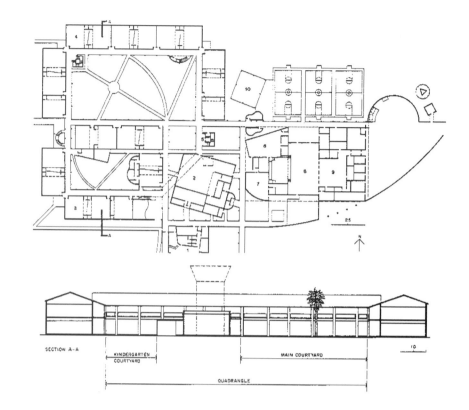

Main entrance.

wing, and an outdoor recreation area—that fan out around the media center. "Three solids and a void," says Romney. Each element was designed as a standard building block that can be easily adapted to a particular site.

Key to Romney's plan are two open grassy courtyards, which allow light and air to permeate all the classrooms. By facing classrooms inward on the courtyards, rather than out on the street, Romney succeeds in creating a sense of community and security. Though the classroom quadrangle appears to be one element, it is, in fact, a pair of buildings, each with its own separate courtyard. The smaller contains the

Classrooms look onto a courtyard.

kindergarten, while the larger holds the upper grades. Linked by covered corridors and stairways, the rooms are discrete units with which students can readily identify.

Romney built flexibility into the plan by pairing most of the classrooms. A common movable blackboard wall hung from a dropped soffit slides on tracks so that the two 34-foot-square classrooms can be made into one large room. The dropped soffit also serves another function: It provides essential space for HVAC units.

The hub of the school is the two-story media center, traversed by an upper-level bridge, which houses a traditional library, a resource room, and a storytelling pit. Its skewed orientation dramatically sets it off from the rest of the project's grid, while serving to underscore its symbolic and circulatory function. From the media center students have access to the service wing, which includes a cafeteria-auditorium, kitchen, music and art rooms, and mechanical spaces.

The most public face of the project is provided by the one-story administration building. Housing the principal's office, support-staff offices, and a teachers' lounge, the building is the only one that protrudes beyond the complex's perimeter. In fact, the school's prevailing sense of enclosure is accentuated by a curving concrete-block wall to the right of the school's two entryways.

The media center comprises a library, a resource room, and a story-telling pit.

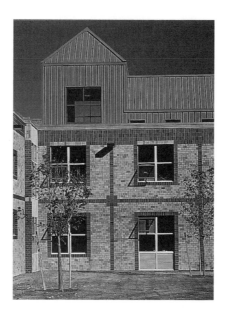

Light monitor brings natural light into the library.

Methuen Comprehensive Grammar School, 1990
Methuen, Massachusetts

HMFH Architects

172,000 square feet

Twenty-seven acres seemed like more than enough land even for a large K–8 school. But when much of the site turned out to be wetlands, HMFH Architects faced a real challenge squeezing a 1200-student school onto the buildable parts of the property. The result is a carefully orchestrated building complex linked to its outlying playfields by a series of outdoor bridges. Critics have likened the school to a castle linked to playing fields by a moat.

To reduce the scale and massing of the building, the architects broke the school down into a series of connected pavilions, some two stories high and others three. The architects varied the roofs as well, mixing steeply pitched gabled roofs with flat ones and pyramid-capped towers.

The school is a series of two- and three-story pavilions.

A similar approach was taken inside the school, where the kindergarten, elementary, and middle-school areas were separated and given their own identity. Central core facilities are organized around a three-story entrance lobby and are accessible to the public after school hours without compromising the security of the classroom areas.

The architects made the most of every opportunity to create memorable common areas. A two-story cafeteria, a sophisticated auditorium, and even corridors that rise two stories show students that this building is special. Perhaps most impressive is the grand library (called the "information media center") whose twin light monitors bring natural illuminate to the room from above.

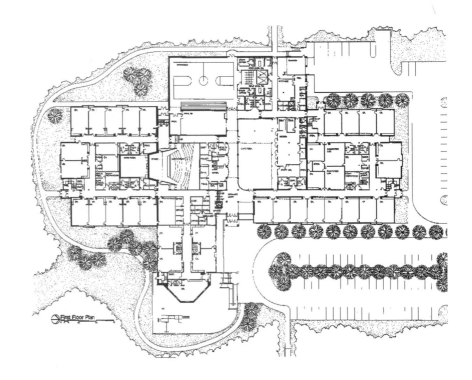

The auditorium.

Buckeye Local High School, 1990
Connorville, Ohio
Lesko Associates, architect
137,300 square feet

A comprehensive high school that replaces three older schools (one of which was destroyed by fire), Buckeye High serves a diverse group of students and residents. Because a primary aim was to serve the community as well as the students, Lesko Associates received a great deal of input from the administration, staff, students, and members of the community.

"We wanted to get away from the feeling that you are institutionalized when you come through the doors," stated superintendent Anne Stephens. "Now when you walk into this school, you have a calm and easy feeling. It's a very relaxed atmosphere." Contributing to that are an outdoor courtyard in the center of the academic area, a dramatic barrel-vaulted library-media center, which is the focal point of the building, and a pyramid-shaped cafeteria-commons.

What determined the building layout was an unusual site configuration—106 undeveloped acres adjoining a river, with a wooded hillside that slopes down to a level flood plain. The linear two-story masonry building, incorporating a variety of geometric forms, was located parallel

Entrance facade.

The strong horizontals on the exterior reflect the school's internal layout.

to the river, well above the flood-plain, and built into the lower portion of the hillside. The setback from the highway affords a dramatic view of the entire $11-million complex.

Organized along a large corridor, or indoor street, the academic areas are distanced from spaces such as the cafeteria-commons, physical education complex, and auditorium that are open to the public. In the academic area, which includes 32 classrooms and functions almost as a separate building, some rooms have motorized walls that allow team teaching of larger classes. An early childhood day-care center is an unusual feature of the home economics area. "Since all the high school students are now in one building, we can offer a wider range of courses," notes Stephens.

The barrel-vaulted library-media center.

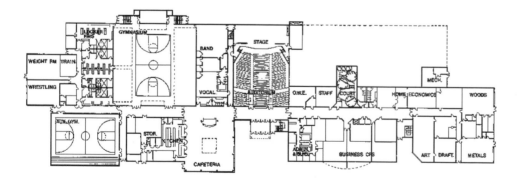

B. D. Billinghurst Middle School, 1990
Reno, Nevada
Lundahl & Associates, architect
115,000 square feet

To encourage interaction between
students and teachers, Lundahl &
Associates designed the B. D.
Billinghurst Middle School around
two major social spaces: an interior
courtyard and a multipurpose din-
ing-commons area. Taking advantage
of the benign local climate, the school
carefully mixes outdoor rooms with
indoor spaces. While more traditional schools establish a strict sepa-
ration between indoors and out,
Billinghurst blurs the distinction.
    The dining-commons area,
located directly behind the main
entrance, is the social focal point of
the $9.3-million school, while the
courtyard just beyond it is the outdoor hub. By making a landscaped
outdoor room so accessible, the

design encourages students "to go outside for a break," says architect Jeffrey Lundahl. Both the commons and the courtyard were designed to be flexible enough to handle small groups and large ones.

The academic focal point of the school is the instructional materials center (library), located on the other side of the courtyard in the middle of the classroom side of the building. One of its many functions is to provide video transmission via two different channels to all classrooms through a sophisticated media network.

In addition to 26 general classrooms, accommodating 1000 students, there are three computer classrooms, four special-education classrooms, and four science labs clustered in their own wing. Specialized classrooms, including art, living skills, drafting, and shop, are also housed in a special wing. A music center is provided with separate band and choral labs near the gymnasium for acoustical isolation. The administrative area is near the front entrance for security purposes, with the faculty lounge adjacent to it.

Because the site slopes 12 feet across the building pad, the one-story school actually has three different floor levels, interconnected by corridor ramps for handicap access throughout. The sloping condition presented some unusual design problems, such as varying wall and roof heights and some tricky ramp transitions at the different levels.

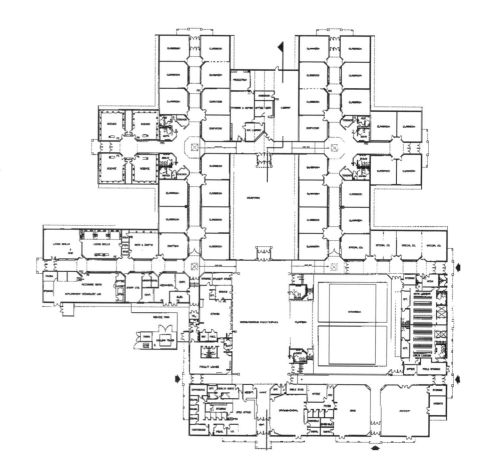

The library is the heart of the academic block.

Building a school is often a major event in a small rural town. Especially if the community envisions using the space for its own activities. Case in point is Hope, Indiana, population 2200, where everyone from school administrators to teachers, parents, and students was eager to be involved in the process.

Yet, what set Hope's experience apart from that of other small towns was its ability to take advantage of the Cummins Engine Foundation's standing offer to cover the cost of architectural fees for public-works projects in its hometown of Columbus and throughout Bartholomew County. After an extensive search involving 10 nationally known architectural firms, Hope selected the Houston firm of Taft Architects. What gave Taft an edge was its willingness to engage the whole community in the design process. Everyone wanted a versatile building that evinced civic pride while accommodating multiple uses. Another requirement was that the school be linked to the nearby high school and playfields.

What Taft partners John Casbarian, Danny Samuels, and Robert Timme developed was an H-shaped plan, with the main entrance opening onto an indoor "main street." The entrance, a portico made of brick-and-concrete courses, introduces the project's most important interior elements—the indoor street, arches framing the street, and the pavilion form. Modeled after European arcades that form a series of storefronts, the interior street features a series of bay windows that visually highlight the administrative offices, the art room, the music room, a math-reading room, and a lounge. To break the long corridor into smaller sections—and to dramatize the points where it intersects the two wings—Taft designed pavilions with

South facade with library.

115

pyramidal skylights and thick masonry piers. One pavilion leads to the classroom wing, while the other feeds into such communal areas as the gymnasium, the cafeteria, and the kitchen. In the classroom wing the long corridor is broken down into clusters of four rooms, with groups of two rooms facing each other across the hallway. That enables teachers to work more closely, if they wish.

Halfway down the main corridor is the library, the symbolic hub of the school. Its octagonal shape is the only element, except the entrance portico, that breaks out of the linear grid. The room is built on two levels—bookshelves line the perimeter while reading tables are set half a level below in the middle.

Taft focused on the child's perspective throughout the design process. One example is how they placed the project's emblematic brick-and-concrete courses on the children's eye level. Classroom windows are set at 2 feet, 4 inches above the floor and extend to 8 feet. "But we weren't restricted to a child's scale," admits

Main corridor.

The library.

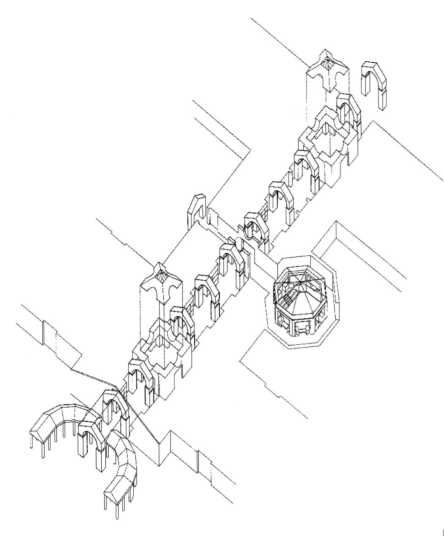

Robert Timme. "We didn't want all of the spaces to feel small." So Taft alternated large with small spaces—the institutional and community areas with the more intimate and residential.

Building the school with a simple steel frame, masonry walls, and a fixed width of 60 feet allowed Taft to stick within the $4.5-million construction budget. "We used durable, inexpensive materials and made them look rich," explains Danny Samuels.

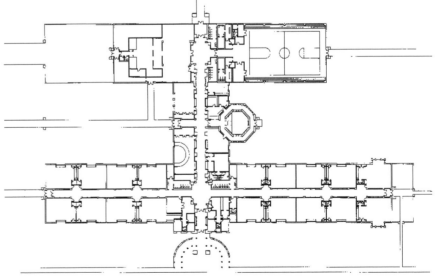

Oak Ridge and Forestdale K–8 Schools, 1990

Sandwich, Massachusetts

HMFH Architects

121,450 square feet

To cope with a rapidly growing population of school-age children, this Cape Cod community decided to build two identical K–8 schools at the same time on different sites. Each school accommodates 780 pupils.

Separate wings for K–6 and grades 7 and 8 operate independently, but share a gymnasium, cafeteria, library, multipurpose room, and music room. This "school within a school" approach provides small, individualized programs for both upper and lower schools without having to duplicate administrative and common areas.

On the outside of the building, distinctive cupolas and towers (which house part of the heating and ventilation systems) act as visual landmarks and help break down the massing of the masonry building. On the inside, two corridors intersect to form an "L," with the major common spaces (such as the cafeteria and large multipurpose room) located near the main entrance. This arrangement provides the community with easy access to the larger rooms after school hours. Movable partitions in the cafeteria and gymnasium give these rooms the flexibility to handle groups of various sizes.

Determined to create a lively environment for learning, HMFH architects used plenty of natural light and bold swatches of color on wall surfaces and architectural trim. The architects also paid close attention to fenestration, bringing windows down to a child's height and opening up the two-story lobby with glazing.

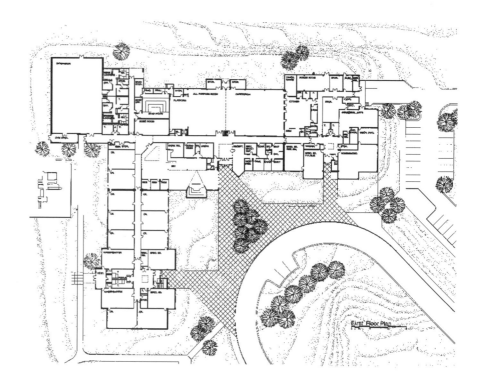

Entry lobby.

Main entrance.

Towers and cupolas help break down the scale of the school and serve as landmarks.

Science Magnet School No. 59, 1990
Buffalo, New York

Stieglitz Stieglitz Tries, architect

135,000 square feet

Attached to Buffalo's Museum of Science and Zoological Gardens, this unusual school serves as a citywide resource for science education. A magnet school that draws its pupils from the entire city (and is part of Buffalo's desegregation efforts), the new building provides classrooms for prekindergarten through sixth grade, as well as a library, administrative offices, cafeteria, and physical education facilities for a science magnet program that includes an existing seventh- and eighth-grade component at the Zoological Gardens. In rethinking standard educational models and establishing strong ties with an existing city institution, this science magnet school may prove to be a valuable prototype for the country as a whole.

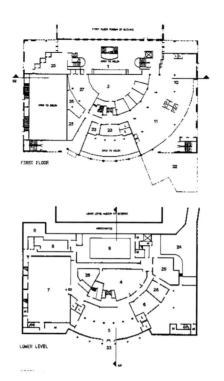

FIRST FLOOR

LOWER LEVEL

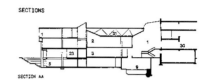

SECTIONS

SECTION AA

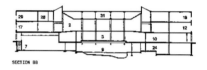

SECTION BB

The new science magnet school has been added to an existing museum of science.

An atrium links old with new.

The cafeteria.

Although it uses different materials, the new building matches the massing and scale of the older museum. Inside, however, the school cuts a very different figure, offering more light and dynamic use of space than its Classical neighbor. Linking the old with the new is a three-story-high circulation atrium in which most of the stone south facade of the museum has been preserved. Visual and physical connections between the museum and the school on all floors (except the below-grade level) ensure that the two institutions truly work together.

Architects Stieglitz Stieglitz Tries placed the major teaching spaces on the second floor and fanned them out around a central library-media center that includes a computer lab and visiting scientist-demonstration lab. A concealed electrical raceway floor system throughout the second story and portions of the first and third stories provides virtually unlimited access to a buildingwide computer network.

The school's lower level contains a complete gymnasium, pool, locker rooms, kitchen, and a cafeteria fronting onto an outdoor amphitheater. The first floor accommodates administrative offices, as well as prekindergarten and kindergarten classrooms. The second floor handles grades 1 through 6, while the third floor takes care of special facilities such as art rooms, ceramics center, music rooms, and technology lab. The top floor also includes an expanded library for the Museum of Science, freeing up valuable floor space in the old building for exhibits.

Warsaw Community High School, 1990
Warsaw, Indiana

The Odle, McGuire & Shook Corp. and
Perkins & Will, associated architects

256,000 square feet

2,000 students

The references to Midwestern farm buildings—such as grain-elevator roofs and silolike staircases—clearly tie Warsaw High School to its rural landscape. But the architects' design for this 256,000-square-foot project is more than a simple essay in regional forms. While farm clusters tend to be ad hoc groups of individual structures, Warsaw High is a deliberately symmetrical campus that marries a formal plan with unpretentious agrarian imagery.

The latest in a half-century-long tradition of innovative school design, Warsaw High School represents a remarkable degree of continuity at Perkins & Will. Ever since it collaborated with Eliel Saarinen in designing the Crow Island School in Winnetka, Illinois, in 1940 (p. 33), the firm has retained its position as one of the most important forces in school architecture. In the past two decades partners William Brubaker and Ralph Johnson have infused a new sensitivity to regional architecture into Perkins & Will's work, picking up on the New Mexican Territorial style at Capital High School in Santa Fe (p. 93) and other Southwestern themes at Desert View Elementary School in Sunland Park, New Mexico (p. 84). Without abandoning the firm's roots in Modernism, Brubaker and Johnson have adapted their designs to fit into local contexts.

Set on the windswept Indiana prairie, Warsaw High is starkly delineated from its surroundings by tall, flat elevations. "I thought of these surfaces as walls protecting the school," says Ralph Johnson. Turned inward, the school is organized around a protected central courtyard, enlivened by a variety of three-dimensional structures that extend out to form covered walkways

The semicircular media center is clearly expressed on the school's south facade.

The school's architecture recalls that of grain silos and other rural buildings.

The school turns inward onto a landscaped courtyard.

and step down to meet protected courtyards.

"The teaching staff made it clear it wanted natural light in all classrooms," recalls Larry Craff, superintendent of Warsaw community schools. In response, a series of rectangular light courts were inserted in both wings facing the courtyard. To bring even more light into the double-loaded classroom corridors, clerestory windows were inserted on the second floor. The most dramatic play of natural light is found in the huge, curving, three-story media center. Ringed with windows, it infuses the center of the classroom wing with sunshine.

The school's main courtyard is divided in two by an enclosed one-story gallery that also connects the building's two wings. The two halves of the school itself fall on either side of the court: classrooms and media center to the south, and gymnasium and cafeteria to the north. Classrooms are grouped by department, with corresponding offices located nearby. The only exceptions are special-education rooms, which administrators requested be integrated with the other classrooms. Also in response to a specific request, administrative offices were decentralized, instead of being grouped in a traditional block.

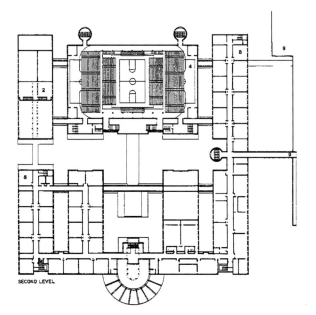

SECOND LEVEL

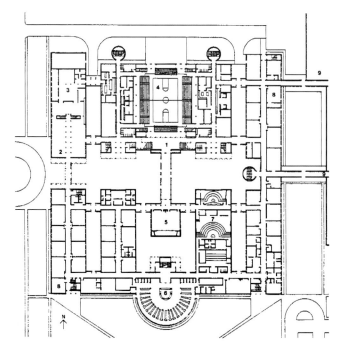

Another requirement was that the school be able to accommodate new technologies as they are developed. Consequently, each classroom was wired for computers and video equipment. An electronic resources room in the media center supplies video programs to classrooms at the touch of a button, eliminating portable VCRs individually operated by teachers.

A 5000-seat gymnasium, which can be divided into seven practice courts, was considered a necessity in basketball-crazy Indiana. Because it acts as an important community facility, it's accorded its own separate entrance off the main court.

Set next to a 60,000-square-foot building that once housed the town's freshman high school, the new building is connected by two enclosed walkways. The school district agreed to recycle the building as a vocational center at the architects' suggestion. Now the building is equipped with industrial technology labs and rooms for teaching such business skills as word processing. The architects were able to keep costs down and project a sense of rural economy by using a straightforward structural system: steel frame infilled with masonry on the lower portion of the building and metal panels above.

The one element that breaks out of the architect's tightly contained "walled city," with all its classrooms focused on the center courtyard, is the spectacular circular library-media center. "We wanted the library to be the most important feature in the most important building in town," states Brubaker.

An entry gate and courtyard form a protected outdoor room.

Stair leading to media center.

Hunt Elementary School, 1990
Puyallup, Washington
Burr Lawrence Rising & Bates Architects
45,975 square feet

Designed as a prototype for a rapidly
growing school district, the Hunt
Elementary School is an adaptable
facility with three major components:
a central core and two classroom
wings. The two-story core—which
houses all common spaces such as
library, administration offices, and
multipurpose room—remains essentially constant, while the one-story
wings adjust to the needs of each
school and its site. As with most prototypes, the Puyallup project aims to
reduce the amount of time and
money it takes to design and build a
new school. If a design works, why
start from scratch each time a new
school is planned?

    Because all of the schools will be
located in residential neighborhoods,
architects Burr Lawrence Rising &

Gables, pedimented porches, and shingles give the school a residential feeling.

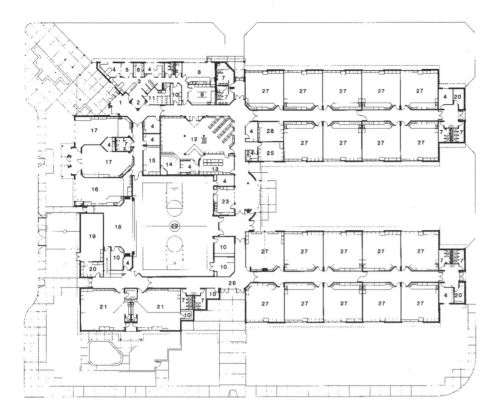

The library.

Bates gave their design a residential feeling with simple gables, pedimented porches, and materials such as stained cedar shingles and brick.

Community involvement was an important part of the school's program, so the architects zoned the building into public and private sectors. Areas that might be open after school hours, such as the multipurpose room and the library, are located in the central core and can operate independently of the classroom wings. The architects also designed separate entrances for the public and students, giving the public entry prominence on the front of the building so visitors know exactly where to come and locating the student entry on the side where buses can pull up.

The architects also paid special attention to making the prototype school as energy-efficient as possible. Insulated windows, translucent skylights, and clerestory windows bring natural light into 90 percent of the building, thereby reducing heating needs. The HVAC system is a unitary water-to-air heat pump with individual units above corridors. The basic components of this system include heat pumps, storage tank, cooling tower, boiler, and water-loop piping. The system takes heat collected in classrooms (due to solar gain, body heat, and lighting) and transfers it through the water loop to cooler areas. Heated water is also stored in a 10,000-gallon underground tank and then used when needed. Controling all these processes is a computer-based energy-management system.

Forest Bluff School, 1990
Lake Forest, Illinois
Booth/Hansen & Associates, architect
10,000 square feet

A one-story Montessori school, the Forest Bluff School offers an alternative education for about 150 children ranging from infants to 12 years old. The simple wood-frame structure features an expansive shed roof covering the building's circulation spine and "great hall" and eight projecting classrooms. The compact plan, in which all of the public spaces are contained in the spine and classrooms line up on either side, establishes a delicate balance between a sense of community and a need for independence.

The great challenge for architects Booth/Hansen was finding an appropriate architectural expression for the innovative Montessori method of education. In particular, the architects had to design classrooms where children often work at their own pace in an unstructured setting, while occasionally attending more formal presentations. The solu-

Each classroom is its own pavilion.

The school features a shed-roofed spine and projecting classroom pavilions.

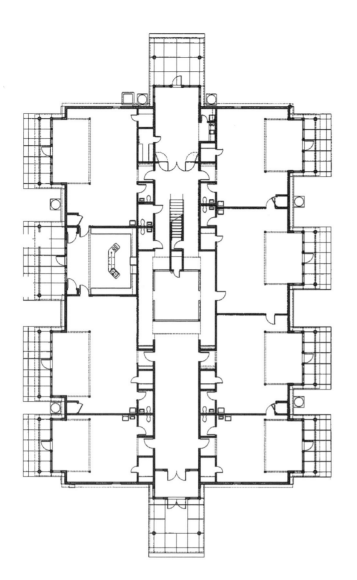

tion that Booth/Hansen developed is a flexible space for independent learning attached to a projecting two-story pavilion used for talks and presentations. The gable-roofed pavilions give each classroom its own identity, a covered outdoor space, and a generous amount of natural light. A mezzanine level above the spine's great hall holds teacher conference spaces and a small library.

The building also expresses the Montessori educators' belief in craft. By exposing the wood members supporting the structure's shed and pavilion roofs, the architects turned the building itself into a lesson in architecture. The school's natural materials encourage students to touch and use all their senses.

The great hall.

Classrooms include space for independent learning and a projecting two-story pavilion.

Minischools, 1990
New York City
Weintraub & di Domenico, architect

The rapid growth of the school-age population over the last decade has put great pressure on cities such as New York to expand facilities quickly. Until recently, New York's standard response was to erect preengineered metal annexes in school yards. When the city was finally forced by a watchdog agency to develop a less dreary solution, it turned to architects Weintraub & di Domenico.

Employing the same type-V construction and corrugated metal as had been used in the past, Weintraub & di Domenico designed a series of four "minischools" whose playful, and brightly colored forms won immediate praise. "We have a knack for making silk purses out of sows' ears," says John di Domenico.

Instead of trying to disguise the humble construction technology,

Pediments and columns are playful additions to preengineered structures.

Although the metal shed remains the same, entry elements vary with each site.

A triumphal arch marks this entry.

the architects worked with it to create a variety of whimsical pediments, portals, and columns that give each building its own identity. "We didn't want to fudge it," explains di Domenico. "We didn't want to just put a brick veneer on a metal shed. So we took the palette of materials that's typical of this building type and shook it up."

The minischools are 60 feet wide with 20-by-20-foot classrooms loaded on either side of a corridor. Each one costs about $2 million and takes about six months to build.

Window detail.

Canterbury Elementary School, 1990
Canterbury, Connecticut

Kaestle Boos Associates, Inc., architect

43,000 square feet

This elementary school for 350 children in grades K–3 is a good example of a design that incorporates regionalism. It also responds well to the needs of children in the early grades. Respect for scale is evident in interior spaces. The height of casework, windows, and doors is designed with children in mind. Changes in texture and color above each door make corridors less expansive. In fact, hallway lengths are minimized, and classroom entries are defined by floor-tile patterns. Corridors are capped with concrete plank, forming an attic where piping, ductwork, and conduit are located. Service and expansion needs may be addressed in this space with minimal disruption to rooms below.

The central lobby, in contrast, is a tall space finished with brick and tile and crowned with a skylight. Not only does it define the school's entry, but it is the terminus of exterior and interior circulation. Closed-circuit

Main entrance.

The school sits on a 27-acre wooded site.

The school's lobby is a two-story space.

television monitors the entry from the office. Extending out from the lobby is a canopy, which shelters students against unpredictable New England weather.

The building's exterior harmonizes with the architectural character of its surroundings in rural eastern Connecticut. Pitched roofs, cupolas, and batten-seam fascias mimic the vernacular style of agricultural buildings that dot the landscape. Set back from the road, the school rests on a knoll carved from 27 acres of woodland.

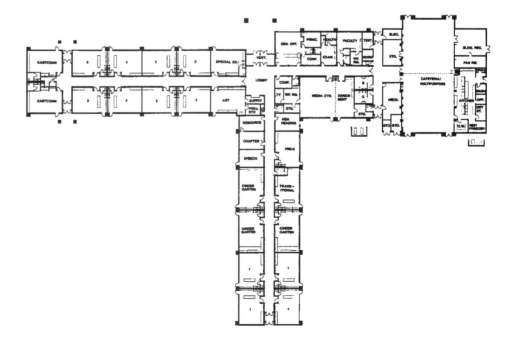

Westridge Elementary School, 1990
West Des Moines, Iowa
RDG Bussard Dikis, architect
84,422 square feet

This West Des Moines school district could not get space fast enough to keep pace with rapid community growth while it was building this school. Because enrollment projections were difficult to establish, the program required a minimum of three classrooms for each grade (first through sixth), two kindergarten classrooms, miscellaneous special-education classrooms, and support spaces. To accommodate future growth, the facility was designed for easy expansion, including six additional classrooms, two kindergarten rooms, and one early-childhood-development space. In fact, the additional six classrooms, initially bid as an alternate, were actually constructed as part of the finished facility. The building contains 84,422 square feet for 740 pupils.

Since the school district had been installing temporary classrooms for use until the new facilities were built, the architect designed the school around the concept of flexible spaces that could temporarily house additional classrooms. Eight class-

Main entrance.

East facade.

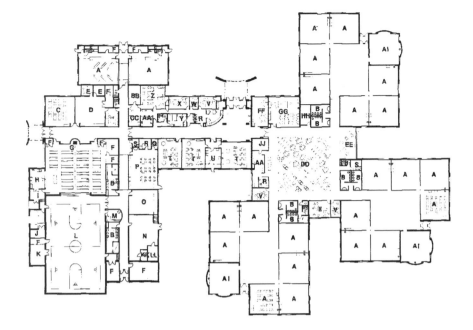

rooms were clustered around a "commons," which functions as the flexible space. It can serve as a small-group activity area, a place for movable coat wardrobes, or a temporary classroom. Three of these classroom clusters, or pods, were constructed in all.

Community use of the gym, community room (a multipurpose lunchroom), kitchen, music classrooms, and art room was anticipated in the program. Zoning of the plan permitted access to these spaces, while the remainder of the building was closed off. The community-use zone was sited adjacent to the primary parking area for easy access.

Because of an unusual site—the land sloped so that adjacent residential property was actually on higher ground—the design of the building's roof was of special concern. Careful massing of the building to create vertical elements, the use of primary colors, and the addition of skylights helped give the metal roof the necessary appeal. Imaginative use of color was continued on the interior.

Library interior.

Child Care Laboratory, 1990
Wake Technical Community College
Raleigh, North Carolina

Haskins, Rice, Savage & Pearce,
architect

16,700 square feet

Wake Technical Community College, which has grown from 34 students in 1963 to over 33,700 students today, wanted to provide practical experience for students enrolled in its early-childhood education program. The design for the resulting Child Care Laboratory, built in 1990, was dictated by the college's educational philosophy that a child's development is related to the quality of his or her environment. Accordingly, the physical space, materials, and various interactions among people should all be dedicated to optimizing the growth and development of the enrolled children.

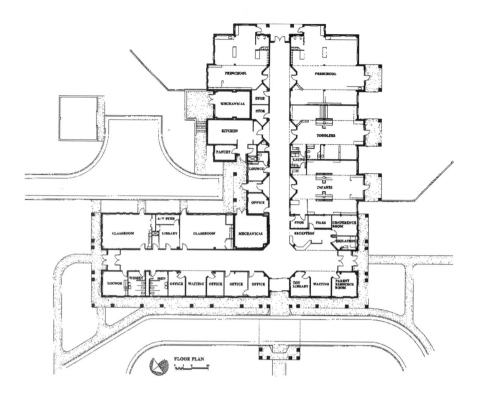

FLOOR PLAN

The school is broken down into a series of gable-roofed pavilions.

Simple geometric shapes enliven the main corridor.

To implement the program, the architects oriented the building along two intersecting axes: the east-west child-care wing and the north-south adult curricula and administrative wing. The main entry and reception area are defined by the intersection of these axes. The child-care wing houses four classrooms—for infants, toddlers, two-year-old preschoolers, and three- to four-year-old preschoolers. The entrance to each classroom is illuminated by natural light from skylights directly above it. Wood trim at the doors and windows is painted a primary color to identify each room. Infant and toddler rooms have specially designed diaper-changing and flushing facilities.

The architects used basic geometric shapes—circle, square, and triangle—throughout the design, notably in the windows and ceiling vaults. In the classrooms all casework, lavatories, toilet fixtures, and so forth are designed at child height. Each classroom has an adjacent covered portico for outdoor play.

The adult curricula and administrative wing houses two adult classrooms, related faculty and administrative offices, and a student waiting area. An unusual feature of the Child Care Laboratory is its toy library, where parents may check out toys for their children's home use.

Oak Brook Elementary School, 1991
St. Louis, Missouri
Pearce Turner Nikolajevich, architect
67,000 square feet

Fondly called "the Roller Coaster School" by students and teachers, Oak Brook Elementary combines a profound concern for its educational program with a more playful expression of certain functional elements. Rather than being something added at the end of the design process, the school's innovative architecture stems directly from the local school district's progressive approach to education—one that still embraces elements of the open classroom plan of the 1960s.

Although the school's distinctive roof may at first seem arbitrary, it is actually an effective means of bringing natural light into public spaces and a powerful way of articulating the building's circulation spine. Because natural light was such an important concern of the client, the architects combined high clerestory windows that supply diffused light with lower windows that frame views of the outdoors and bring in direct sunlight. Inexpensive masonry such as split- and ground-face concrete blocks form the building's base and its larger masses (including the gymnasium and library), while lighter materials such as corrugated-metal siding and glass reinforce the hovering roof forms.

Architect George Nikolajevich organized the most important public

A "roller coaster" roof brings sunlight into the school's circulation spine.

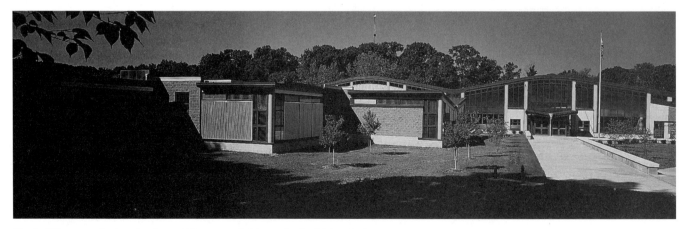

The building was designed so it could be expanded into a junior high school.

Clerestory windows help light the library.

spaces (administration offices, cafeteria, art room, library, and gymnasium) along the circulation spine and then grouped classrooms into two clusters on opposite ends of the school. As a result, the plan breaks the 600-pupil institution into two minischools—one for kindergarten through third grade and the other for fourth through six grades—with shared facilities in between. In the K–3 educational cluster, four classrooms for each grade level surround a multipurpose room, giving each grade its own focus and identity. For the older students, the architects used an open-plan approach in which each grade level consists of four teaching stations in one large space plus an attached "project area."

Flexibility was a key concern of the client, so the architects designed the school with a repetitive 30-foot module that allows nonstructural walls to be easily moved. By placing mechanical and electrical systems in the ceiling, the architects ensured that all conduits and connections would remain accessible even if interior partitions are moved. The school board also asked the architects to consider possible changes in the district's demographics and prompted them to draw up expansion plans that would allow the building to change from an elementary to a junior high school.

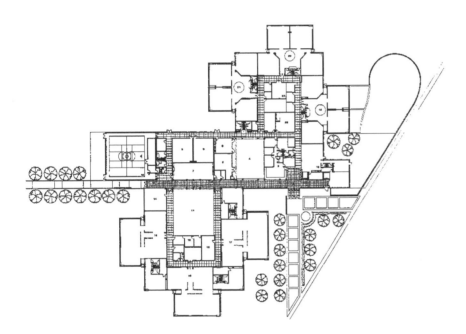

Circulation spine.

P.S. 233, 1991
Queens, New York

Gran Sultan Associates, architect

17,500 square feet

New York's first school dedicated
solely to handicapped children, P.S.
233 goes beyond the purely functional needs of its special population
to provide a bright, cheerful environment that plays an important role in
supporting the learning taking place
there. An economical steel-frame
structure with lightweight metal
trusses and steel-stud walls, the
building serves 100 of the city's
most severely retarded multiple-
handicapped students ranging in age
from adolescents to young adults.

The school's mission is to help
these students become as independent as possible, teaching them basic
living skills such as self-grooming
and eating with utensils, as well as
fine-motor skills that might help
them qualify for simple-assembly
jobs. To provide a reassuring setting
for the students and to fit into a
neighborhood of single-family
houses, the school is a one-story
building with a residential character.
An attic provides space for all of the
building's mechanical systems.

Designing a barrier-free building was just one part of the school's
demanding program, explains architect Warren Gran. To make the
school as inviting and light as possible on the inside, Gran and his associates used clerestory windows, large
glass-block openings that provide
security without metal screens, and
generous classroom windows that
sometimes extend all the way to the
floor. The large windows give students on floor mats and in
wheelchairs views outside. The
architects also convinced the New
York Board of Education to increase
the size of the classrooms so that an
area in each room could accommodate wheelchairs and therapeutic
equipment. Brightly colored, well-lit
corridors not only provide enough
room for ambulatory devices, but create a playful setting for the informal

The building is an economical steel-frame structure.

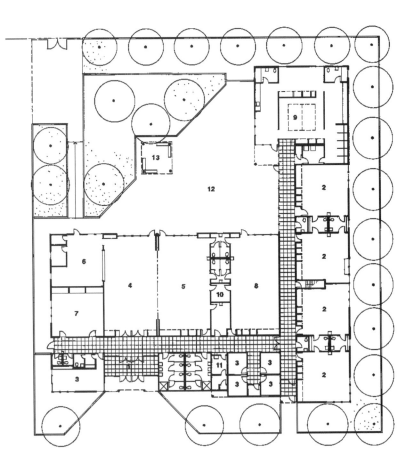

conversations that often start up when slow-moving students and their teachers move through the space. One of the school's best traits is that it doesn't look as though it was designed for the handicapped. Move the wheelchairs out of the way, and a visitor would be hard-pressed to identify the building as a facility devoted to a population with special needs.

Clerestory windows bring natural light inside.

Interiors have a residential tone.

Worthington Kilbourne High School,
1991
Worthington, Ohio
NBBJ, architect
272,000 square feet

Set on what had once been a 55-acre farm, this sprawling high school takes full advantage of its wooded site. A ravine that runs through part of the site provides much of the natural drama, as a covered open-air walkway crosses it on the school's first floor and classrooms bridge it on the second floor. To make maximum use of this water feature, the architects surrounded it on four sides, forming an outdoor courtyard that brings light and views indoors.

Serving a bedroom suburb of Columbus, the 272,000-square-foot school has as much of a residential character as is possible of a building this size. Sloped roofs, dormers, and residentially scaled windows help the structure fit into its neighborhood of single-family houses and break free of an institutional image. The school's placement in and around the ravine at the site's lowest elevation also helps buffer it from the adjacent neighborhood.

The 1500-student school is clearly a reflection of its community's commitment to education. Costing $29.3 million, the facility includes a 13,000-square-foot library, a 750-seat auditorium, a 2000-seat gymnasium, and a 21,000-square-foot auxiliary gym. A two-story-high commons room adjacent to the dining area provides a grand space for students to relax and congregate, while also offering spectacular views of the woods. All shared facilities, such as library, dining, administration, and gym are located on the first floor, connected by a mall-like corridor. The school's 55 classrooms, various science labs, and computer rooms reside on the second floor.

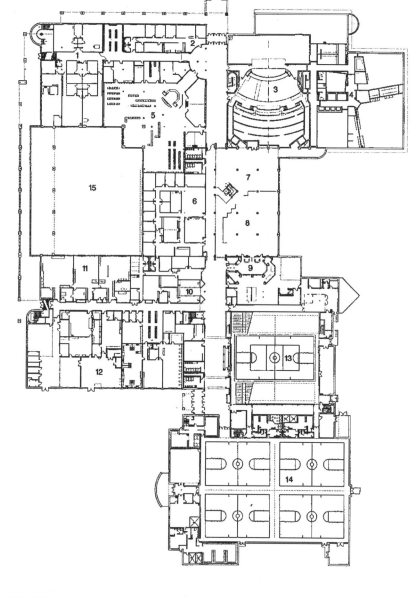

The courtyard.

Sloped roofs help reduce the apparent mass of the school.

The commons is a grand space with views to the courtyard.

The school bridges a ravine.

Perforated metal awnings protect windows on south facade.

Snaking flat roof projects beyond classrooms on north facade.

Like many older schools throughout the country, Mt. Carmel Elementary needed to expand and renovate. Dating from the 1930s and 1950s, the two-building school outside Atlanta was far behind the times in terms of facilities and amenities. After razing one of the school's buildings, architects Lord, Aeck & Sargent performed more than just a face-lift. Quite simply, they executed a complete transformation of the nondescript brick structure into a sinuous complex pulsating with energy and color. In fact, the metamorphosis is so complete that it is hard to find the old building, on either the inside or the outside.

Encouraged by the local school board to be innovative, the architects designed a new 31,000-square-foot building with a wavelike metal roof that crests in the center above the gym, then slides down to smaller spaces at either end. The rolling roof not only provides the extra height needed for the gym and "cafetorium," but it turns the main corridor into a vibrant street punctuated by treelike columns on one side and a band of clerestory windows on the other. Treating the two sides of the corridor differently makes sense since one leads to public spaces such as the gym, cafetorium, music room, and media center, while the other leads to a classroom wing sheltered by a low flat roof whose snaking edge extends beyond the building. A load-bearing concrete-block structure, the new building sports an eclectic collection of exterior material, including colored concrete block, stone, and aluminum-coated metal shingles. The architects specified textured materials as a way of encouraging students to touch and explore the building. The designers also exposed the ceiling's metal bar joists and steel roof and painted them bright colors to show students how the building was put together.

In the old building, the architects installed new windows, perforated-metal sun shades, and the same metal shingles found on the new building. Inside they added new ceilings made of perforated and corrugated aluminum and replaced all mechanical and electrical equipment. To dress up the front of the building and provide a covered place for students to wait for buses, the architects designed a sawtooth perforated-metal canopy cantilevered above brick piers. With its energized form and exposed construction, the canopy is an appropriate introduction to this reborn school.

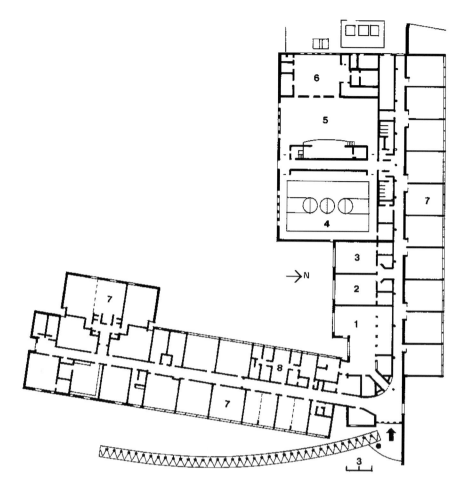

New windows, sun shades, and aluminum shingles dress up the old building (*left* in photo).

Metal canopy covers children at bus stop.

Main corridor.

Employee Day Care Center, Ingalls Memorial Hospital, 1991
Harvey, Illinois

O'Donnell Wicklund Pigozzi and Peterson Architects

9000 square feet

Built in response to the need of the staff of Ingalls Memorial Hospital for a private day-care center, this facility can accommodate 120 children, ranging from infants to toddlers and preschoolers. The facility is located on a site directly across from the hospital entrance, making it easy for staff to visit their children during breaks. It also offers visitors and employees a friendly welcome to the hospital and it provides a much appreciated break from the hospital's more pressing concerns.

Exterior materials such as brick and limestone were used to match those of the nearby hospital.

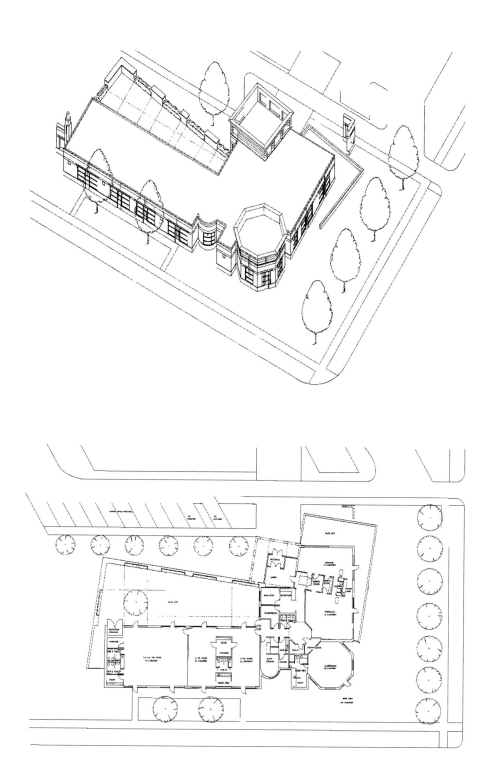

The design of the 9000-square-foot facility with an L-shaped plan provides flexible activity space for infants and toddlers in one wing and areas for preschoolers in a second, larger wing. A shared octagonal multiuse room anchors the corner. The multiuse room, planned as a large motor-skills area, was designed with support space so that it could function as a future activity room, if required. In response to a tight budget, shared support spaces—such as food preparation, restrooms, and staff areas—were incorporated into the facility between activity rooms.

The exterior of the free-standing facility was designed to fit with the hospital and surrounding buildings. Brick, limestone, and synthetic stucco were chosen to match the recently completed hospital building directly across the street, providing an integrated campus setting. Exposed-steel lintels over the windows recall similar forms used in the nearby hospital. Building configuration was also influenced by contextual issues. The massing of the day-care center calls attention to two prominent features: the entry pavilion and the multiuse room. Raised areas of synthetic stucco on both of these structures reinforce their identities and act as screens, concealing the mechanical rooftop units from the nearby patient bed tower.

The L-shaped configuration addresses a security issue by creating a defined campus edge to the adjacent residential neighborhood to the east, while adding a sense of privacy to the center's outdoor play area. The octagon-shaped multiuse room is designed as a distinct pavilion to note its special use and have it act as a hinge turning the corner. The eastern facade is further broken down into smaller building elements to help reduce its overall massing along this residential street.

University High School, 1991
Orlando, Orange County, Florida
W. R. Frizzell Architects, Inc.
270,000 square feet
2023 students

A prototype high school in Orange County, Florida, University High resembles a Spanish village, complete with a central plaza, arcades, and small courtyards separating buildings. Colored stucco and red-tile roofs enhance the Mediterranean character of the school.

A triple arch in front of the main plaza marks the formal entry to the school and its most public facilities. Shared functions such as the gymnasium, dining hall, auditorium, and administration offices surround the arcaded plaza, while classrooms spread out to the north or occupy the second floor. Equipped with 85 classrooms, the school offers a diverse curriculum including instruction in business, computers, agriculture, marketing, performing arts, government, sciences, social studies, and languages.

The school also features such sophisticated new facilities as a closed-circuit television production studio and a performing-arts center that includes a 900-seat auditorium. Special vocational-education centers include an agricultural complex, an athletic department with dance studio, weight rooms, and a 2000-seat gymnasium.

Courtyards and tile roofs give the school a mediterranean character.

The school's auditorium seats 900 people.

The central plaza serves as a focal point for the entire school.

Stuyvesant High School, 1992
New York City

Cooper, Robertson & Partners and
Gruzen Samton Steinglass, associated
architects

406,000 square feet

The first new high-school building in
New York City in 15 years,
Stuyvesant breaks new ground in
several ways. Not only is it located in
Battery Park City, the much-
acclaimed mixed-use neighborhood
built on landfill in southern Manhattan, but it towers above most other
schools. Instead of spreading out
along the ground, a luxury unafford-
able in Manhattan, Stuyvesant rises
10 stories high and will certainly be
studied as one of the first examples
of the high-rise high school.

Like the Bronx High School of
Science and Brooklyn Polytech,
Stuyvesant is one of New York's well-
respected magnet schools specializing
in math and science. Formerly
located on the east side of Manhattan
in an aging set of buildings, the
school was lured cross town by the
promise of new facilities and a com-
manding site in an emerging neighborhood. Certainly, the budget was
generous with $95 million earmarked
for constructing the 406,000-square-
foot institution. But the program was
equally grand, calling for 71 classrooms, science labs, a 900-seat auditorium, an indoor swimming pool,
two gyms, art studios, a cafeteria, a
library, administrative offices, and
computer rooms. In addition, all
classrooms are hooked up to a
sophisticated telecommunications
network and the entire school is air-
conditioned and handicapped-
accessible. Like many new schools
today, Stuyvesant is to be used by the
community as a whole, not just students. As a result, facilities such as
the swimming pool and the auditorium are on the ground floor and can
be operated at night and during the
summer when the rest of the building
is closed.

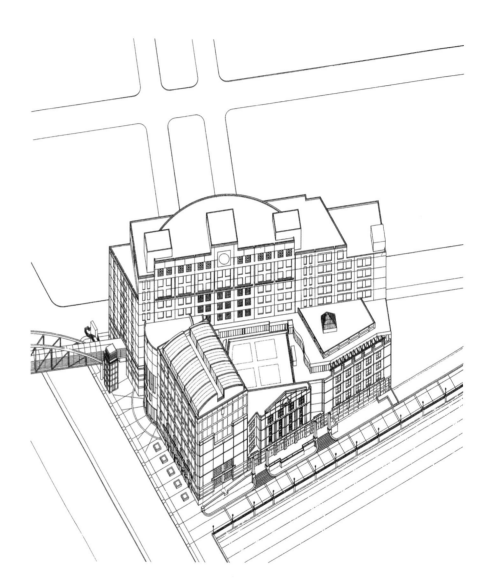

North facade.

South facade.

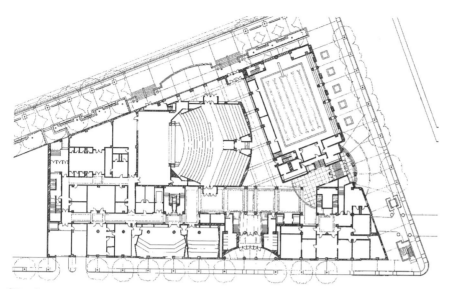

Because the school rises 10 stories, the two architecture firms hired to design it—Cooper, Robertson & Partners and Gruzen Samton Steinglass—had to rethink the issue of circulation. The solution developed by the architects is a system of skip-stop escalators that supplement stairways and allow all students to get to their destinations within four minutes.

Stuyvesant's location on a 1½-acre triangular site encouraged the architects to treat each of the school's major facades as a separate composition. The south facade, looking toward the rest of Battery Park City, is the most symmetrical and flat of the three. The north elevation, which addresses the Hudson River, breaks down into three distinct blocks (sports center, theater, and shops), thereby reducing the apparent bulk of the structure. On its east elevation, the school also reads as a tripartite composition—two wings attached to a central academic tower.

Clad in brick and limestone to respect its nineteenth-century neighbors, the new Stuyvesant High School is scheduled to open in the fall of 1992.

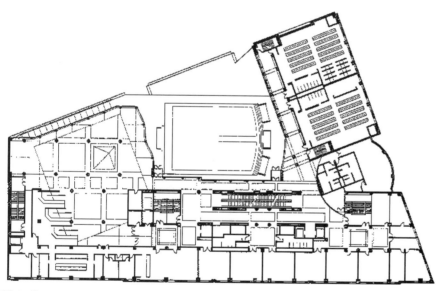

Main floor.

4

The Future

While no one can predict the future, we can get at least a blurry picture of what's to come by looking at what has already begun. So it is with school design. To a large degree the emerging trends in school architecture will be continuations of current concerns: accommodating community needs and new user groups, minimizing the impact of large facilities, and giving individual schools their own identities. The future, though, will also be shaped by trends that are just now beginning to be recognized: incorporating new technologies, planning for year-round education, and responding to a more localized decision-making process.

There is also a movement in the country aimed at equalizing educational opportunities. With a number of books and studies highlighting glaring contrasts in the quality of schools serving rich and poor, the judicial system has become more active in demanding changes. As a result, many states are reexamining the way they fund school construction, trying to find alternatives to the local property tax. Although the situation is still in flux and varies from state to state, it is clear that more attention—and perhaps more money—will be paid to schools in less affluent areas.

One response to demands for parity of school facilities might be greater dependence on prototype schools. Although they are often developed for other reasons (such as greater efficiency, speed of construction, and reduced overall costs), prototypes might serve as acceptable common denominators for both rich and poor areas.

Just as schools are becoming community resources open to a broader spectrum of users—adults as well as children—so, too, are they responding to the needs of more specialized groups. Schools today include facilities for abandoned children, children with learning disabilities, and children learning English as a second language, to name just three types.

Discussed below are just a few of the important trends likely to influence school design over the next 10 years. Many of these trends can also be seen in the projects shown in the second half of this chapter, projects currently on the boards.

Rendering of the Perry Community Education complex (*opposite*).

Smaller Is Better

Almost every teacher believes that students perform better in smaller classes. As a result, parent groups and state legislatures are pushing for regulations that limit class size, especially in elementary schools. The ideal class size is probably around 20 pupils, although guidelines in some states allow for classes of up to 30. The impact on school design is clear: Schools have to get bigger. Two classrooms for 20 pupils each require more space than one for 40 pupils. Floor plans must also respond, by either extending corridors or somehow grouping classrooms in clusters. The challenge for architects is to find ways to organize a growing number of classrooms without making schools feel like bureaucratic mazes of cells. Related research is also showing that students perform better in smaller schools. The Public Education Association, a private advocacy group in New York City, points out that the most successful schools are private schools—small institutions usually with enrollments of no more than 500. Size is particularly important in economically disadvantaged areas and cities, where students often feel no attachment to (and have little respect for) their school. Understanding this, the Public Education Association, in conjunction with the Architectural League of New York, organized an exhibit of designs of small schools for actual sites in New York in 1989. Fifty-nine architectural teams responded with detailed plans for schools that fit into their dense urban contexts and create a sense of intimacy and caring.

Educators have debated the question of school size for decades. How big should a school be? The answer, of course, depends on the kind of school envisioned, the surrounding community, the age of the pupils, and a host of other factors. Perhaps the best answer is the one Harold Gores, head of the Educational Facilities Laboratories, used to give: The proper size for a school is one where the principal knows the name of every student.

Smaller class sizes, specialized facilities for particular groups of students (learning disabled, gifted, foreign, etc.), and increased community use, however, are forcing schools to expand in size. Because of land acquisition costs and economies of scale, building two small schools will almost always be more expensive (and time-consuming) than building one large facility. In a time of government budget deficits, it is becoming increasingly difficult to get the extra money for smaller schools. One design response that shows promise is creating "schools within schools," shaping smaller environments within larger institutions. Whether the architect does this by breaking down a school into various "houses," each with its own identity (and sometimes even its own entrance), or by some other means may be less important than the general response itself. The lesson is that design approaches do exist that can mitigate students' perception of size. A large school does not necessarily have to be a numbingly anonymous one.

Designing for Technology

While architects have long considered the technological needs of building types such as offices, studying the best ways to provide electrical and cabling capabilities to workstations and computer rooms, for example, they have just begun to examine the electronic needs of schools.

One school project that squarely addressed the issue of new technology is the expansion and renovation of the Penn High School in Osceola, Indiana, in 1989 (p. 91). A districtwide commitment to the use of technology in education guided almost every aspect of the project's design and execution. The technology consultant on the project, Dr. Ray L. Steele, of Ball State University, told the planners involved with Penn High School: "The school environment . . . will provide an electronic information and communications infrastructure allowing information exchange experiences and homework assignments of a more complex and varied nature. . . . Classroom experiences will be enriched by electronic delivery of audio or data-based information from sources throughout the world. That could easily and cost-effectively include special courses unavailable in the local curriculum." Dr. Steele went on to describe a future that may not be very far away: "The most basic technology may become the portable student work station, a device which will combine characteristics of the personal computer, a videodisc player, a video cassette recorder, a word processor, and a telephone. It will plug into a campus nervous system allowing on-call access to an array of information sources which can be delivered virtually anywhere at very minimal cost."

Schools of the future, which include ones like Penn High that already exist, must therefore provide the wiring and cabling facilities for such technology. As a result, architects must ensure that each classroom—indeed, each desk and teacher station—be hooked up to a schoolwide electronic network. This network will provide interactive video and data transmission within the school and between the school and outside sources. Distance learning—a practice that allows students to "attend" classes via computer hookups—is already a reality in some parts of the United States and will become a standard method of teaching in the future. Distance learning will not only allow people in isolated areas or those who are homebound to continue their studies, but it will greatly expand the educational offerings available at any one school. If a student in a small town, for example, wants to learn Swahili, he or she might be able to attend a nationwide class by computer.

The Year-Round School

Proponents of year-round schools point to a number of different benefits: better utilization of existing facilities, alleviation of overcrowding, and accommodation of community use. Whatever the reason for its adoption, the year-round school requires architects to address a variety of needs. These include the following:

- *Orientation.* Architects must consider how both summer and winter conditions affect the building. For example, windows must be located or designed so they are protected from direct rays from summer sun.

- *Larger facilities.* Meeting rooms, auditoriums, staff rooms, and conference rooms may be needed to accommodate a variety of different groups. Additional space for administrative and support staff may be needed.

- *Outdoor spaces.* Shaded outdoor eating or teaching areas may be wanted for summer use.

- *Extra storage space.* Multitrack schedules may require extra storage space for the additional teachers using the school.

- *Durable materials.* Year-round use will require more durable materials and finishes.

- *Air conditioning.* In most parts of the country air conditioning will be required for summer use.

- *Energy use.* Because facilities will be used in both hot and cold months, schools will require more sophisticated energy-management systems and a building envelope that reduces heat loss and gain.

- *Landscaping.* Trees and other landscaping elements that shade buildings in summer months may be cost-effective and attractive ways of reducing energy consumption.

Prototype Schools

Because the planning, design, and construction of a school is such a time-consuming and expensive process, some localities have explored the use of prototype designs. Once a design is developed and then approved, it could be used at different locations without having to go through the entire process each time. Most school districts experimenting with this approach allow for certain changes on each project to accommodate different needs and site conditions. But the concept remains the same: If a design works, why not save money and energy by using it again?

While prototypes are currently a hot topic, they are not exactly new. More than 25 years ago, New York considered using "stock plans," going so far as commissioning architects to develop plans for a variety of school types (an elementary school for 750 students, a comprehensive high school for 1500 students, and another high school for 2500 students). Specific sites were not selected, so designs tended to be more generalized than perhaps desired. Ultimately, none of the stock plans were ever built. In the 1960s California experimented with a School Construction Systems Development project that devised systematic design and construction methods for building new schools. A number of such schools were indeed built.

Prototype designs raise a host of issues. Some of the considerations architects and educators must address when developing prototype schools include the following.

- Because of site variations does program suffer? Are spaces compromised to fit the system?

- Does the tendency to design blocks of space force program to fit a module?

- Can prototype designs respond to different neighborhood characteristics?

- Recognizing the realities of the construction industry, will real savings result?

- Will contractors find the prototype process more or less attractive than the current one?

- Will prototype schools be more or less responsive to changes in interior space needs and changes in educational philosophy?

- Does the prototype approach restrict design creativity, resulting in "cookie cutter" schools?

The most sophisticated and advanced prototype school program now under way is in New York City. In 1989 the city commissioned four architecture firms to develop prototype designs. Today 13 schools, based on these four prototypes, are now nearing completion, right on schedule. [The projects are discussed in more detail on pp. 163–174.] All of the architects involved in the program and many outside observers are pleased with its results so far.

How much time and money has been saved and how successfully the program might be expanded remain to be answered, though.

Magnet Schools

Programmed for specialized curricula (such as the sciences, the arts, or a particular vocation), magnet schools were developed to draw students voluntarily from a citywide area. Originally created in the 1950s and 1960s as a way of breaking through traditional patterns of racial segregation by bringing together students from all parts of a metropolitan area, magnet schools today are popular with a broad spectrum of the public. As particular subject areas become increasingly complex and the facilities required to teach them increasingly sophisticated, demand has increased for schools that specialize in a limited field. The trend to magnet schools seems to be gaining speed all the time.

While early magnet schools adapted themselves to existing facilities, most of them today feature buildings designed specifically for their needs. Sophisticated science labs and computer equipment, for example, are important elements in the new Stuyvesant High School, a magnet school geared to teaching math and science, nearing completion in New York City (p. 152). Perhaps the best known magnet school in the country is New York's School for the Performing Arts, the subject of both the movie and television series "Fame." In cities around the country, schools devoted to aviation careers, the humanities, computer sciences, international studies, health professions, and business are now in operation. In 1991 Dade County, Florida, opened a design and architecture senior high school.

Privately Operated Public Schools

Dissatisfied with the quality of students graduating from America's public schools, some private corporations are beginning to take matters into their own hands. Arguing that businesses would do a better job of building and operating schools than the current maze of educational agencies and school boards, some people are now advocating that cities privatize education the way some have already privatized garbage collection, street maintenance, and other essential public services.

In May 1991, Christopher Whittle, the head of Whittle Communications of Knoxville, Tennessee, made headlines by announcing that his company planned to build a chain of 200 schools nationwide. Estimating that each school would cost $15 million to build, Whittle said he was ready to spend $3 billion on the program. A couple of years before, Whittle had caused a ruckus launching "Channel One," a television news program beamed directly to schools and supported by commercials. Although Whittle donated sophisticated television equipment to each of the schools that signed up for "Channel One," many people argued that commercials for soft drinks and snack foods had no place in school.

Whether Whittle goes ahead with his ambitious plans for privately run schools or not, it is clear that many people are dissatisfied with the current system of delivering educational facilities. Although no one knows now how a privately built school would differ from the ones governments build, the approach is based on the idea that they would indeed be different and better.

The following schools are currently on the boards or under construction. Although hardly inclusive of all important trends in school design, these projects highlight some of the directions in which architecture for education may be headed.

Portfolio of Projects Still on the Boards
New York City Prototype Schools Program

After years of neglecting its existing schools and forsaking much of its responsibility to build new ones, New York City initiated a program in 1987 to build 189 new schools over the next 10 years. Spearheaded by a newly formed School Construction Authority empowered to cut through much of the local government's bureaucratic red tape, the program has proved to be both surprisingly efficient and innovative. A major element in the city's effort to build fast is the school prototype program, which commissioned four well-respected architecture firms to develop flexible, modular designs that could be built on a variety of sites. As Rose Diamond, the deputy director for management at the Board of Education's division of school buildings, explained, the idea was to develop "a 'kit of parts' rather than a 'cookie-cutter' approach." As of mid-1992, the first generation of prototype schools—13 buildings based on four different designs—was nearing completion, right on schedule.

Prototype Elementary School, 1992
New York City
Gruzen Samton Steinglass, architect
76,000 to 93,000 square feet
600 to 900 students

Designed for three sites in northern
Manhattan, this prototype is based
on four different modules that can be
assembled in a variety of ways. The
kit of parts includes the following.

• A multistory classroom module
  accommodating 300 students. All
  classrooms and offices are located
  along perimeter walls and have operable windows. Projecting bay windows in each classroom define special
  educational zones and provide long
  vistas down city streets.

A design with three classroom modules.

- A commons module that includes all long-span spaces such as auditorium, lunchroom, and gymnasium. Designed to work as a separate structure, this component can function independently of the rest of school during after-school hours.

- An administration module that consolidates teacher-support areas, administration offices, and specialized program spaces. Located in the center of the school, this component acts as a control zone between the classroom and commons modules.

- A connector module containing lobby areas and vertical circulation and inserted between the classroom and administration components. While providing the building with a distinct entry point, this module also allows the other components to join in various directions and levels, responding to specific site conditions and needs.

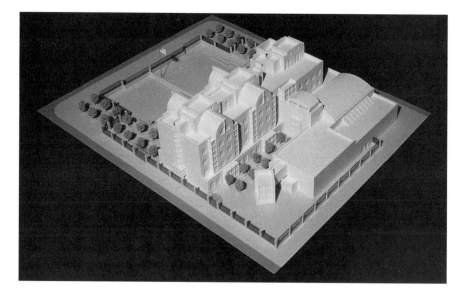

A school with two classroom modules.

A school in the Sherman Creek neighborhood has three classroom modules and an administrative block lined up on one side of the commons module.

For a tight site on West 204th Street, the architects placed the commons block behind the classroom and administrative modules.

Model shows commons block on the left and classroom and administrative modules on the right.

Prototype Elementary School, 1992
New York City
Perkins & Will, architect
77,000 to 96,000 square feet
600 to 900 students

Given the same basic program as Gruzen Samton Steinglass, Perkins & Will also developed a design based on four functional components. But while Gruzen Samton Steinglass modeled their design after New York townhouses, Perkins & Will took their cues from Modern sources, employing a stripped-down esthetic sympathetic to the Art Deco character of the Bronx neighborhoods in which their schools would be built. The functional components in the Perkins & Will prototype are as follows.

• A four-story classroom/teaching cluster for 300 students, including regular classrooms, special-education classrooms, and teacher work areas.

• A four-story administration-resource tower, including administrative offices, a teacher's lounge, a library, and shared resource space for art, science, and computers.

• A community center composed of a two-story lunchroom-auditorium.

• A one-story gymnasium.

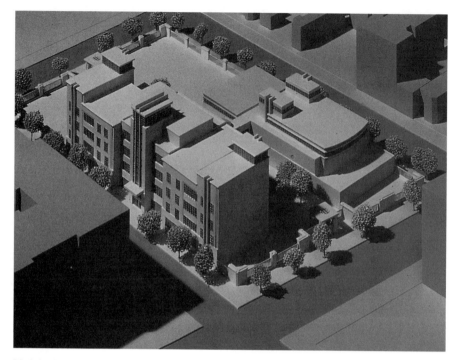

Model of LaFontaine Avenue School shows administration tower flanked by classroom blocks with lunchroom-auditorium module in the rear.

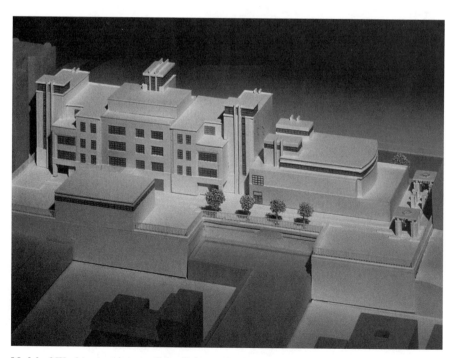

Model of Washington Avenue School shows the interplay of four-story and two-story elements.

Rendering of the four-story administration-resource tower.

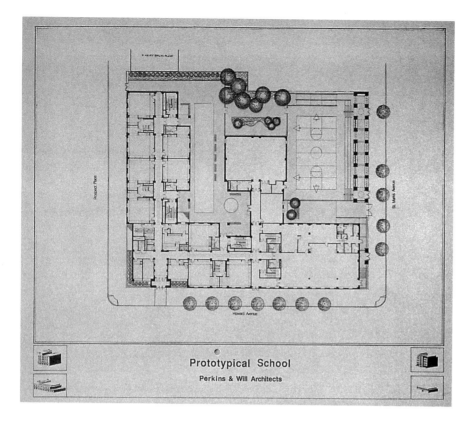

Prototypical School

Perkins & Will Architects

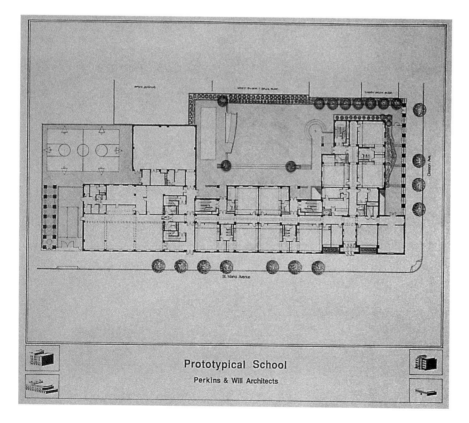

Prototypical School

Perkins & Will Architects

Prototype Elementary School
New York City

Ehrenkrantz, Eckstut & Whitelaw, architect

131,816 square feet

1200 students

In the early 1960s, Ezra Ehrenkrantz helped conceive the California-based School Construction Systems Development project, an experimental program to devise systematic design and construction methods for new schools. His involvement in SCSD is reflected in his 1200-student prototype, which was built on two sites in Queens and one in the Bronx. The components of this scheme include two identical, four-story classroom modules that each accommodate 550 students; a two-story block for 100 special-education students enrolled in a program for the disabled; an administrative wing containing offices, guidance counseling, a medical clinic, and a library; and a gymnasium-auditorium.

To distinguish each module with a strong individual identity, the architects housed the functions within a series of gabled bays. While

Gabled bays help distinguish each module.

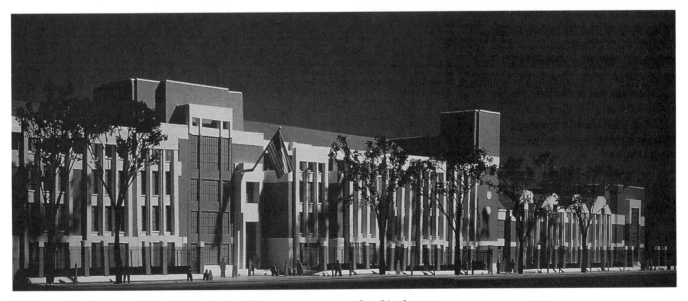

In this version classrooms look onto the street while common areas are placed in the rear.

the school's main entrance is through
the administration wing, each classroom module also has its own
entrance. The links between the various wings have been custom-
designed so that the modules can be
placed at different angles to accommodate specific site conditions. These
corridor links are fully glazed,
thereby offering views to courtyards,
play areas, and adjacent streets.

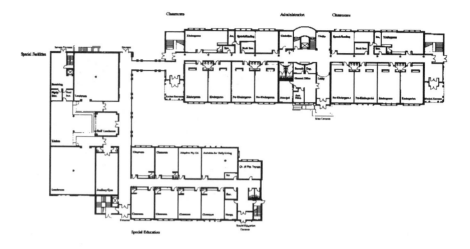

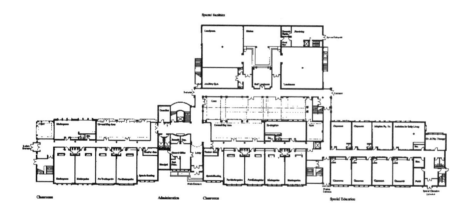

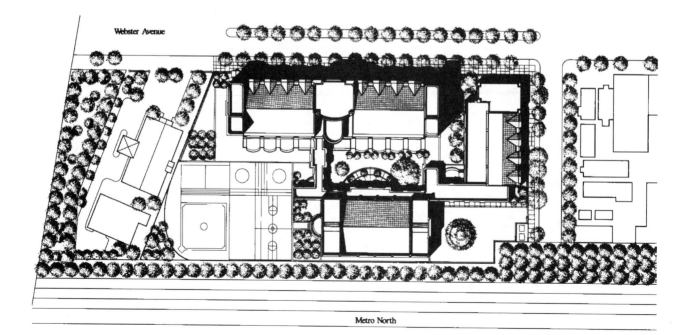

The school embraces a landscaped courtyard.

A glazed circulation link helps turn the corner.

Prototype Intermediate School
New York City

Richard Dattner, architect

106,000 to 169,000 square feet

900 to 1800 students

Assigned an intermediate-school program to be built on four sites in Manhattan, Queens, and Brooklyn, Richard Dattner designed a prototype that consists of just three components: a pair of identical classroom modules for 550 students each, a third classroom module for 600 students, and a centrally located structure containing shared facilities such as administration, gymnasium, and lunchroom. Special-education classes for the most acutely disabled students are integrated throughout the school.

The two 550-student classroom modules are curved forms that help differentiate them from the rest of the school and give them their own identity as subschools. The building's strong cornice lines and decorative brickwork are intended to be reminiscent of the Collegiate Gothic imagery of the public schools built by New York City at the turn of the century.

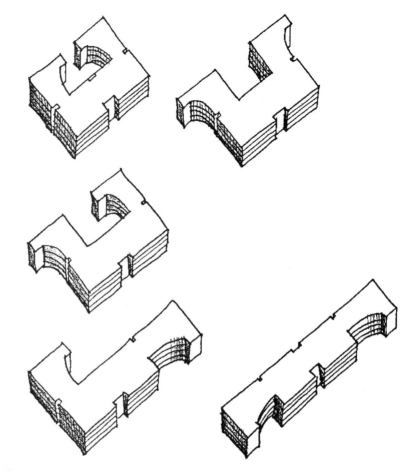

Variations on a theme.

Strong cornice lines and decorative brickwork are reminiscent of Collegiate Gothic schools of a previous era.

This prototype comprises curved classroom wings and a shared facilities block that adapts to the site.

Locally Managed and Designed Public Schools in California

Although first used to give neighborhoods more control over the curriculum and management of their schools, site-based management has now begun to affect the planning and design of schools as well.

North facade.

Jean Parker Elementary School
San Francisco, California

Reid & Tarics Associates, architect

36,000 square feet

570 students

The Jean Parker Elementary School in San Francisco's Chinatown is an example of how one architecture firm successfully responded to the movement for more local control or site-based management. According to Charles Schrader, of Reid & Tarics, the school's principal and members of the Chinese-American community played a vital role in the planning and design of the building.

The design challenge here was to develop a school on half a city block that would meet today's educational needs, provide adequate play area (both open and enclosed), accommodate off-street parking, and

View from the south.

serve the needs of the dense, urban, Chinatown community. The 570-pupil elementary school, which replaces a 1910 facility torn down after the powerful 1989 earthquake, includes 15 classrooms, two kindergartens, a multipurpose room, a library, a science room, and below-grade parking for 19 cars. The seismically reinforced school is organized into three distinct building masses: classrooms, administration, and a community-school multipurpose room. The building elements are placed around a south-facing courtyard-play area, providing protection from the cool winds that sweep the site year-round.

The three-story classroom building is placed away from the busy frontage road, and the classrooms are further buffered from traffic noise by core facilities of restrooms and stairwells. Each classroom has bay windows containing window seats in keeping with the Bay Area tradition. The administration building recalls the former school in its classical proportions and use of materials. A large terra-cotta portal salvaged from the demolition is the building's focal point. On the second floor above the administration offices is a two-story library with 22-foot ceilings and tall bay windows. A separate trellised entry sets off the multipurpose room, making it suitable for major community events.

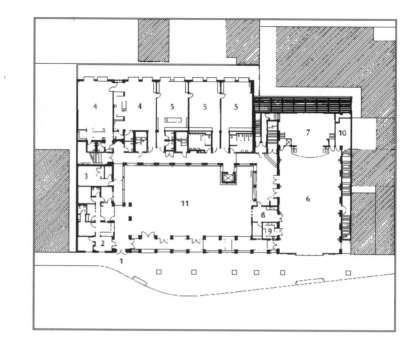

Santa Ana High School Addition, 1993
Santa Ana, California
Reid & Tarics Associates, architect
88,000 square feet (addition)
3700 students (total facility)

The school will blend old and new elements into a cohesive campus.

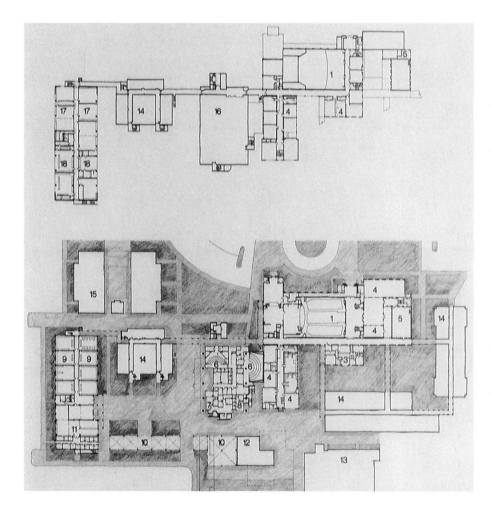

Although started in 1986, the expansion and reorganization of Santa Ana High School will probably not be completed until 1993. A joint effort of the city's redevelopment agency and the local school district, the Santa Ana High project is intended to help revitalize the old downtown area where the school is located. In conjunction with the school expansion, the city has cleared a number of blocks of slum housing to create a new civic complex and has upgraded First Street to become a handsome boulevard.

A large school with more than 3700 students, Santa Ana High began with a couple of Art Deco buildings dating from the 1930s. Other buildings have been added over the years, the most recent in the mid- and late 1960s. Each of these structures has its own entrance and sense of identity. Over time, the main circulation developed at the back side of the buildings, forming an external circulation network that functioned for both service vehicles and pedestrian use. Almost all the areas between and behind the buildings were asphalt-paved, with only minimum landscaping.

To pull the disparate buildings together, the architects drew up a master plan that organizes the school into a cohesive campus. All buildings will now look onto a plaza, properly landscaped with textured paving and plantings. The placement of two new classroom buildings at the east and west ends of the axial spine also helps define and limit the internal campus organization. Two direct entrances to the mall are provided off campus at the southern parking lot. Inspired by the Art Deco design of the original buildings, the architects borrowed some of the old masonry and metal detailing, as well as the 1930s color palette, for their new two-story reinforced-concrete structures.

An Education Park in Ohio

The "education park" concept received some attention in the 1970s, but its potential has yet to be realized. The idea behind the education park is to group several schools together in a campuslike setting so certain facilities (such as playfields, gymnasium, auditorium, dining hall, and library) can be shared. Instead of building an elementary, intermediate, and high school on separate sites, each with its own playfields, gym, and so forth, a community puts the schools together in one park. By eliminating the duplication of expensive facilities, the community is able to invest in quality rather than quantity. Instead of having three schools each with a small library, for example, the town can build one campus with a truly impressive library.

Perry Community Education Complex, 1993 (Phase I)
Perry, Ohio

Burgess & Niple, with Perkins & Will, associated architects

677,000 square feet

4500 students

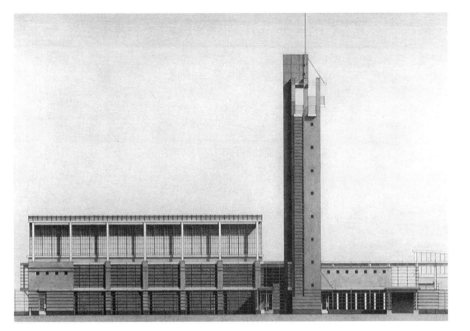

A clock tower serves as a visual landmark.

This enormous project is a 1990s version of the education park. When a local utility company offered to fund a 160-acre educational complex in exchange for approval to build a nuclear power plant, the town of Perry, located east of Cleveland, accepted the deal. When finished, this ambitious project will provide the entire community—both adults and students—with a campus of 677,000 square feet.

The complex consists of two primary zones organized on either side of Red Mill Creek, which diagonally crosses the site. The zones are joined by a bridge-circulation spine and surround asymmetrical courtyards. One zone contains the high school and physical education facility-community fitness center; the other contains the elementary and middle schools. Because the design is based on a system that interacts with the

Major shared facilities such as the gym and auditorium are identified by large curved roofs.

natural features of the site, the organization is fragmented and results in an asymmetrical plan.

The complex is planned to be constructed in phases. The first phase includes the high school, the physical education-community fitness center, and the central physical plant for the entire complex. In the second phase the elementary and middle schools, maintenance facility, and additional physical education facilities will be constructed.

The complex building program is broken down into a limited number of discrete and repeating parts. The parts are defined by different scale versions of extruded shapes with curved roofs. Identifying features include lofts for classrooms and office sections, columnar halls for dining rooms and lobbies, and clearspan halls with large curved roofs for the pool, multipurpose and activity rooms, auditoriums and competition gymnasiums. Circulation and support facilities are identified by flat roofs. The architects also designed specialized elements for more specific functions. For instance, clock towers are singular forms that mark entrances, and fan-shaped library-arts wings contain educational functions different from those housed in the loft elements.

When completed, the educational complex will spread out on a 160-acre site.

The auditorium.

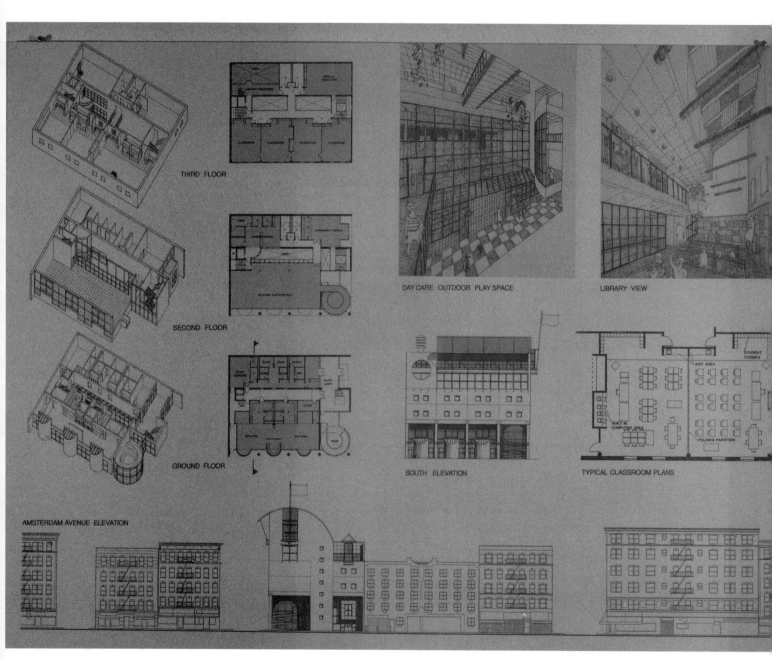

THIRD FLOOR

SECOND FLOOR

GROUND FLOOR

DAY CARE OUTDOOR PLAY SPACE

LIBRARY VIEW

SOUTH ELEVATION

TYPICAL CLASSROOM PLANS

AMSTERDAM AVENUE ELEVATION

5

Delivering the School:
What Every Architect and School Administrator Should Know

An analysis of the projects presented in this book indicates that all are the result of good planning practices. Each is part of a long-range plan of districtwide facility needs. Each building is the result of educational specifications developed to guide the architect in designing space for well-defined educational needs. It is essential that all the players know their roles. There are certain guidelines that should be followed for any capital improvement program. This chapter will discuss the responsibilities of the client and the architect. In some instances the responsibility of each is well defined. In other instances, the process becomes a team approach where all concerned should be involved.

Basic to any capital improvement program is the development of a needs assessment or long-range plan. The plan should include a projection of enrollments, an analysis of all existing facilities, and an exploration of options for meeting both short- and long-term space needs. The decision should be made early on whether to prepare the long-range plan with in-house staff or to contract for the services of a consultant. The elements needed in a successful long-term plan and how to work with consultants will be discussed later in this chapter.

One of the most important decisions the school administrator will make is the selection of the architect and when to bring this professional into the planning process. Clients should understand that a contractual relationship is a two-way street. There are things the client should reasonably expect from the professional, but there are obligations the architect has a right to expect from the client. This chapter will attempt to clarify this issue.

In all probability, most architects invited to present their credentials to a school board are well qualified for the proposed design assignment. Too often, though, the final selection is made on personality, not ability. This is sometimes because in the interview the architect fails to put the firm's strong points forward so that the interviewing group can understand them clearly. A few tips to a successful interview are also discussed later in this chapter.

Once the architect has been awarded the contract, the challenge is to clearly understand the client's educational philosophies and the community's aspirations for the educational environment. Too often the real client is overlooked: the child who will attend the new facility. "What do little eyes see?" One way to approach that problem is to photograph a school from the perspective of a six-year-old.

The educational specifications discussed later in this chapter are an important element of planning. They should not be used as a crutch just to meet space needs. Rather, they should be used to translate the required spaces into places of joy. In educational specifications this author always adds a note to the architect that says "Give me a few surprises." Today's school is not a simple building type.

One of the most important issues involves technology and how it affects school design. Another area often given major consideration is furnishing and equipping the building. The projects illustrated in this book have been looked at in their totality—interior as well as exterior. Security is a prime issue. The challenge is designing a facility that understands security needs without making the school a foreboding, unfriendly place. Closely related is the design of playfields at elementary and secondary schools. These areas are now places for community use. They are not locked up or off limits after school hours.

Understanding the major phases of the building project and who does what will go a long way to ensure the success of a building program. This chapter offers guidelines for the school administrator and the architect.

The School Administrator

Every school administrator should be aware of the seven stages needed to plan a building project, which EFL identified in a study under a grant from the Mott Foundation. The process was designed for community involvement, but it has application for any project.

1. *Get started.* This is not always easy. This is the time to define problems and goals, identify concerns, and most importantly, develop a plan for planning.

2. *Gather information.* A solid foundation of information is essential. This stage includes an examination of enrollments, historical trends, current trends, and projection of future student enrollments. In addition, an inventory and technical evaluation of all existing facilities needs to be conducted. A capacity and utilization analysis should be made of all existing facilities.

3. *Identify priority needs.* Many of the needs will surface from the information gathered in stage 2, but others may surface as the community becomes aware of your activity (for example, need for cooperation with social services agencies, concerns of minority populations, need for use of technology).

4. *Define program requirements.* This is a two-phase process: (*a*) attention to the physical needs—repair, replacement, and new facilities and (*b*) the preparation of educational specifications for all building projects.

5. *Explore options.* On the basis of program requirements, are there options to meet needs consistent with the community's educational goals? For instance, is grade reorganization an option in using existing facilities better? Are there other places in the community where specialized educational programs can be delivered?

6. *Refine the plan.* Go into more detail on the option(s) determined to be feasible. What is the cost? Will district attendance boundaries need to be changed? Can the program be phased?

7. *Follow through.* Present the plan to the community for approval. Have necessary expertise—architects, educational consultants, financial advisors—on board to help present the program to the community.

Long-Range Planning

Gathering information (item 2 in preceding list) and defining program requirements (item 4) are two critical areas of long-range planning that require special skills and techniques. The services of in-house staff or an educational consultant are usually needed to supply the essential facts and figures that the school administrator should use in decision making. Understanding in a general way how enrollment projection, forecasts, capacity and utilization analyses, and evaluation of existing facilities work can aid the school administrators in the overall planning process.

Enrollment Projections

The principal methodology used in enrollment forecasting is known as the *cohort-survival method.* The basic technique requires calculating the ratio of the number of students in one grade in one year to the number of students who survive the year and enroll in the next grade in the following year. This survival rate is calculated using historical membership data. It is affected by such factors as net migration, school promotions, and withdrawal rates. Fluctuations in the data from year to year create a pattern from which an average survival rate can be calculated to project future student enrollment. For example, if over a period of several years, an average of 96 percent of the student membership in grade 3 goes on to grade 4 and if 70 children are now enrolled in grade 3, then next year's grade 4 may be estimated at 96 percent of 70, or 67 students. These average survival rates then need to be adjusted on the basis of specific growth assumptions for each attendance area and local growth data.

From this data, individual school enrollments can be projected. To support the data, the planners need to present a series of charts and graphs on various demographic subjects (employment, population age) that will enter into interpretations. The data should be updated annually to spot any serious variances from the estimates. Then the reasons can be determined and long-range plans adjusted accordingly.

Forecasts

Average daily attendance is the statistic generally used for enrollment projections because it is responsive to a number of factors indigenous to the school and community. Among these forces are promotion policy, annual birth rate, available housing situation, local and regional employment, family size, age structure of population, nature of school services, withdrawals from school, and in- and out-migration.

Although average daily attendance provides a sound, reliable basis for projection, it is not the daily operation level at which school organization and facilities are required. Average school membership is known to be about

5 percent above daily attendance, and normal month-to-month fluctuation of enrollment requires an additional 5 percent of pupil stations over the average membership.

Capacity and Utilization Analysis

There are various methods for determining capacity and utilization. The method presented here is easy to understand and can be kept updated on a spreadsheet. A complete, up-to-date inventory of space in each school building is useful for several management purposes, especially for measurement of school plant capacity as a factor in facility planning and needs projection. The standard unit for capacity measurement of school facilities is the number of work stations to pupils, termed "pupil stations."

The space inventory contains a lengthy list of specialized rooms: gymnasiums, large library-media centers, resource activity rooms, laboratories, vocational rooms, fine-arts rooms, music centers, lecture rooms, and other specialized areas. Some of these rooms will include pupil stations, while support spaces (such as recreational facilities) will not.

The available classrooms and total pupil stations may include portable buildings at some school sites. However, portables should be excluded when summarizing "permanent" facility assets. Total current pupil stations is the gross sum of pupil stations in all instructional areas, as measured by the accepted standards. Permanent pupil stations, however, is the calculated sum of all available pupil stations located in permanent buildings, excluding portable buildings and substandard spaces considered unsuited for instructional use. Accordingly, the current permanent operational capacity is calculated on the basis of the permanent or "net" number of pupil stations. The net operational capacity is a more reliable estimate for evaluating future space needs.

In the utilization analysis, a simplified form can be used to obtain much of the needed data. On this form the current enrollment during each period or hour of the school day is recorded for each instructional room. Instructional rooms are defined as rooms having assigned pupil stations. Such statistics can be used as a precise measurement of the degree of capacity utilization. For example, the space inventory form displays the daily utilization ratio of enrollment to pupil stations for every instructional room in the building inventory.

Experience has demonstrated that when space is in demand, the optimum utilization of permanent pupil stations can approach 85 percent in high schools, 90 percent in middle schools, and 95 percent in elementary schools. Full utilization of this permanent operational capacity can be achieved without instructional damage and is widely accepted by consultants nationally, although it should be noted that a few planners now use 75 percent for high schools, 85 percent for middle schools, and 90 percent for elementary schools. These planners rationalize that new programs, population mobility, and other factors have decreased utilization possibilities.

Evaluation of Existing Facilities

Measuring the gross amount of school facilities, such as square footage of buildings or number of rooms or type of special rooms, is inadequate for determining actual school plant capacity and its usability. A more exact description of physical features, educational features, and site features is required. Accordingly, an on-site survey of the entire school plant must be made and analyzed in terms of building capabilities and needs. As with capacity and utilization methods, there are several approaches used to evaluate the physical plant. Most architects or planners have developed methodologies for facility evaluation. One such instrument, developed by the author and his long-time associate, Wallace Strevell, is illustrated in Table 5.1.

The survey instrument is used to rate a facility on a theoretical 1000-point value score and to weigh different aspects or features of a school plant. Experience over the years with surveying school facility conditions shows that buildings scoring 900 to 1000 are in excellent condition. Buildings that score 700 to 900 are acceptable, but their components parts must be studied; often some alteration or renovation is necessary to put them in first-class condition. When scores are 600 to 700, the buildings have substantial need for rehabilitation and upgrading. If scores are between 400 and 600, conditions are so bad that a complete restudy is indicated. Experience has also shown that when scores fall below 400, speedy abandonment is the only economical or justifiable course.

More than half the total value score of 1000 points (550) is assigned to the educational features of a school plant; instructional rooms have a possible value score of 150; special areas, 250; and operational features, 150. Special areas are further subdivided into special rooms (70 points), general areas (140 points), and administrative spaces (40 points). Given enough space in a well-designed, durable building, a solution can generally be found for special area deficiencies.

How to Use an Educational Consultant

It is a safe bet that on the shelves in school district offices around the country a large percentage of consultants' reports remain unread. These dust-catchers represent untold hours of staff and community time. What went wrong from consultation to implementation? More to the point is how could this waste be avoided. An analysis of some successful client-consultant relationships indicate pointers that show the correct path to follow.

Other points can be added to the list that are directly related to particular problems in a community, but these nine can guide a district in turning a consultant's recommendations into reality.

1. Help the Consultant Understand the Problem

This may seem basic, but it is the roadblock to proper implementation in all too many cases. For instance, in one district an architect spent many hours developing a report on alternative uses for an old elementary school only to be told at the end that an earlier citizen's report recommended the abandonment of the facility in favor of a replacement school. The board gratefully accepted the consultant's report and placed it on the shelf to gather dust. If the architect had known of the citizen's report the option of saving the building could have been one possibility, but recognizing community sentiment would have carried substantial weight on this point.

2. Get Staff and Community Involved with the Consultant

With few exceptions, successful programs result from community participation. This user input is essential, even though it may well be that what the community thinks they want is entirely wrong. If staff and community

Table 5.1 **School Plant Evaluation**

Structural Features

Building structure

	RATING Value 100	SCORE
Condition of foundations		
Condition of exterior walls		
Condition of windows		
Condition of roof		
Condition of floor structure		
Condition of interior walls		
Condition of ceilings		
Plan type		
Appearance		

Safety and circulation

	RATING Value 80	SCORE
Type and condition of stairs and stairwells		
Location of stairs		
Corridor width and location		
Condition of corridors		
Number and location of exits		
Fire and panic protection		
General safety		

Mechanical Features

Air conditioning and heating

	RATING Value 40	SCORE
Type and condition of heating plant		
Heating system		
Cooling system		
Ventilation system		
Temperature efficiency		
Ventilation efficiency		
Mechanical room		
Controls		

Plumbing facilities

	RATING Value 40	SCORE
Toilet room adequacy		
Toilet room conditions		
Water facilities		
Drinking fountains		
Individual room installations		
Showers and special equipment		

Table 5.1 (*Continued*)

Electrical services	RATING Value 30	SCORE
Power installation and control		
Communication and signal system		
Alarms and exit lights		
Special room installations		
General room installations		
Electrical safety		

Illumination	RATING Value 30	SCORE
Number and type of fixtures		
Quantity of illumination		
Quality of illumination		
Controls		
Effect (brightness balance)		

(Value scores are judgmental and independent of the rating of each line item.)

Educational Features by Area

	Location, size shape, capacity (seating for public and special areas)	Type and condition of walls, floors, and built-in features	Furnishings and equipment	RATING Value 150	SCORE
Instructional rooms					

Table 5.1 (*Continued*)

Special rooms	Location, size	Type and condition	Furnishings and equipment	RATING Value 70	SCORE
Music					
Arts and crafts					
Agriculture					
Shops					
Homemaking					
Business					
Science					
Language arts					
Other laboratories (including computers)					
Other space					

General areas				RATING Value 140	SCORE
Auditorium					
Gymnasiums and dressing rooms					
Library or learning resource center					
Cafeteria and food service					
Corridors and foyers					

Administration rooms	Location, size	Type and condition	Furnishings and equipment	RATING Value 40	SCORE
General office					
Principal's office					
Special offices (specify)					
Counselor center					
Health center					
Faculty offices					
Faculty rooms					
Work room					
Other offices (specify)					

Table 5.1 (*Continued*)

Operational Features

Efficiency

	RATING Value 150	SCORE
Suitability for educational programs		
Flexibility		
Economy of effort		
General storage		
Instructional storage		
Pupil lockers		
Acoustical conditions		
Custodial facilities		
Energy system		
Physically handicapped		

Site Features

Site adequacy and development

	RATING Value 130	SCORE
Location		
Size		
Efficient plot plan		
Playfields:		
Size and shape		
Surfacing and drainage		
Equipment		
Safety		
Suitability		
Access to site		
Service roads on site		
Traffic conditions		
Parking (teacher, student)		
Landscaping		
Condition of walks, fences, lighting		
Environment and utilities		
Neighborhood		
(This record is basis for school plant factor profile.)	RATING TOTAL 1000	TOTAL SCORE

become part of the planning process, it is easier to change that attitude and the solution becomes their solution and not that of the outsider.

A classic example occurred in a large city where reorganization and upgrading of all the district's schools were contemplated. Terminology got in the way of the dispute regarding middle school versus junior high. The consultant failed to realize the opposition to "middle school," and the entire program was defeated by a vocal minority that felt left out of the planning process.

3. The Weight of the Consultant's Report Is Critical

Generally, the value of a consultant's "working document" is conversely related to its weight. A voluminous, dull, forbidding report is rarely read or understood. This causes mistrust and results in little or no implementation. Therefore, in addition to a detailed, technical report, a separate report should highlight the most important conclusions in easily understood prose or simple diagrams. This makes the next point vital.

4. Clearly Define Options

Defining options is somewhat like ordering from a Chinese menu. What are the possibilities from "column A" and "column B"? Which are the items, like egg rolls, that are extra? With a clear, simple explanation of the options and their implications, the implementation decision is much easier to formulate and misunderstandings can more easily be avoided. Dealing with options is one way of explaining to the press what's possible. When questions arise, the technical document becomes the reference manual.

5. Involve the Consultant on a Continuing Basis

One of the most frustrating things for a consultant is to be cut off from the project just as implementation begins. Much of the enthusiasm for a project comes from the consultants and it makes sense to keep them on board during the implementation process, if for no other reason than to avoid misinterpreting their recommendations.

6. Revise the Suggested Plan of Action

Even our astronauts have learned to pick up a hammer when in-flight practice varied from computer-based theory. Compromises and minor (or even major) changes are not unusual when a plan is being implemented. If the consultant is part of the implementation team, adjustments can be suggested that will not seriously alter the ultimate goal. For example, if it becomes obvious that the community will not vote in the entire package at one time, phasing should be used to meet short- and long-term goals.

7. A Specific Plan Is Essential

Those dust-catching shelves may also be filled with reports dealing in generalities. Education seems to attract more than its share of rhetoric. The worthwhile consultant is the one who transfers the district's stated desires into concrete educational programs and space recommendations needed to house those programs. If the educational consultant has invented a new language (probably not even understood by the consultant) or the architect finds new words to describe old processes, beware. If you don't really understand the language, the community certainly won't, either.

8. Identify Staff Expertise to Implement the Plan

One of the tragedies is where an excellent plan of action is indicated, but there is no in-house staff to run it. It is part of the consultant's job to indicate what staff commitment is necessary. Sometimes this expertise is available in the district. Sometimes new staff must be brought on board. In one district the consultant team outlined a general plan, but the bulk of the report was a job description for a person to head the operation. Members of the team remained available on a per-diem basis to help the director establish the project office and gradually withdrew with all activities centered in house.

9. Be Realistic about Economic Restrictions

A plan that is so "pie in the sky" as to be economically unrealistic is worthless. We all have to make compromises, and the consultant who does not recognize this is not only worthless, but dangerous. Implementation can occur if the plan is geared to the district's ability to meet the financial requirements not only to start the program, but to maintain it. Architects have long pointed out to their clients that the original building expenditure is minor compared to the long-term cost of maintaining and staffing the facility.

Writing Educational Specifications

"Write good educational specifications. If you don't describe what you want to go on in the building, how can the architect put an envelope around it? He'll do the architecture if you'll do the education," read one of EFL's first major reports.[1] The key phrase is to "describe what you want to go on in the building."

Today writing good educational specifications—educational programs—is more important than ever. Prior to World War II, planning a school building was relatively simple. An elementary school included a series of classrooms, each housing 25 to 35 pupils, an office for the principal and secretary, a multipurpose lunchroom, and a physical education room that doubled for performance and assemblies. In contrast, the elementary school of today has an office suite housing a principal, an assistant principal, a secretary, an office aide, counselors, a school nurse, one or two administrators of federal programs, a conference room, a workroom, and a teacher's lounge. In addition, the classrooms are often mandated as to the number of pupils (for example, 22 in K–4 in Texas). Other spaces include a library-media center, an art room, a music room, a gym (often for community use, too), a "cafetorium," a computer room, and other specialized space for the gifted and talented and for Title I, disabled (physically and mentally) students, and so on.

As schools have accepted an increasing number of responsibilities (drug education, sex education, bilingual education, and so on), the need for more carefully prepared educational programs has become even more essential. Today, there is also a move to site-based management that can only increase the need for written programs that reflect the unique demands of each neighborhood and community while keeping within budget constraints.

The content of the written program can be quickly summarized. A brochure published by the AIA Committee on Architecture for Education, for example, offers six questions that need to be answered when compiling building requirements for a new facility, alterations, renovations, or a long-range plan. The process is adaptable to planning educational facilities at any grade level.

1. *Why is a building program being considered?* Perhaps the reason is an enrollment increase or decrease. In practice, more than one answer to the "why" question is indicated. Other reasons can include the need for specialized facilities, the desire to upgrade the environment of a tired building, the replacement of an outmoded facility, or any combination of these or other reasons.

2. *Who will use the facility?* How many and what age groups need to be housed now and in the future? Are there any special age-group-relationship considerations? Will the facility planned today be converted to another use in the future? For instance, if a school planned as a high school will serve as a middle school at some future date, there may be implications for conversion of spaces. Anticipatory planning can simplify later remodeling.

3. *What subjects will be taught, and how often will classes meet each week?* All subject areas, such as required, elective, enrichment, and special education, must be listed. In addition, adult education or community use of the space must be defined. A projection of the future should be considered, including what changes are likely to occur, such as new, revised, or discontinued subject areas. The "what" stage is the time to dream a little. An educational consultant should try to get those involved in the process to look beyond the obvious and current programs. Compromises, based on limited human resources, both human and financial, can be made later.

4. *When will the space be used?* Today, there is much discussion of year-round schools. Going to a full calendar year has an impact on space and space relationships, as does the need for an extended schoolday, summer programs, community use of the facilities, and other departures from the traditional.

5. *Where will the building be located?* Unless an existing facility is involved, this poses important considerations. Is it to be primarily a neighborhood school, or will busing be involved? Will the site be planned in cooperation with the park district? The architect should be involved in site selection.

6. *How is education to be delivered?* Will it be a traditional classroom setting? Will independent study be an important element? Will a combination of spaces be needed? If so, how many, and how do they interrelate? What will the teacher/student ratio be? The AIA task force suggested that the client should write a description of a typical day or week.

The development of education specifications is the time when the school district or institution should state or revise

- The mission statement.
- The philosophy of education as it relates to the teaching and learning process.

- The desired environment for learning.

- The funds available for the project.

The educational program for the New Orleans Center for the Creative Arts (NOCCA) provide an excellent example of staff and community involvement in the process. The 30-member committee involved in developing the program for this facility included the area superintendent, the principal of NOCCA, a panel of NOCCA teachers, a group of parents of NOCCA students, community members interested in NOCCA, central office support staff, and a board member. A number of subgroups met to discuss specialized concerns: dance, music, theater, visual arts, writing, counseling, social workers, clerical staff, librarians, custodians, and adjunct faculty. In addition, special consultants were retained to explore needs in art, theater, and dance.

In addition to the elements of a good program outlined earlier, the final specifications included the following:

- An introduction explaining the process used in the development of the final program.

- A history of NOCCA from its beginning in a temporary space to its present location in an old elementary school. Also included are the mission statement, goals, and objectives of NOCCA.

- School characteristics, including academic requirements, an enrollment history and projection by subject area, and a profile of the student today.

- General design implications addressing such areas as the use of technology, special lounge and locker requirements, and performance and gallery areas.

- Space-relationship outlines of the unique requirements of NOCCA.

- A complete and detailed summary of space needs that included a detailed description of each space and how it would be used, suggested area for each space, special considerations for each space, and required equipment and furnishings.

As the process progressed, architects were chosen and they took part in many of the planning sessions. While the NOCCA project is a specialized one, the process is appropriate to any project. As stated in the introduction to the NOCCA specifications: "The educational-specifications [program] document is a vehicle of communication between the educator and the architect; the educator identifies the educational objectives and suggests general facility needs; the architect bases his facility design on this information."

Selecting an Architect

The architect should be part of the long-range planning. In fact, his or her services are an essential component in the planning team. The architect can offer valuable suggestions and documentation based on the specialized expertise and experience she or he brings to the project. However, one of the most important points to remember is that the architect cannot be expected to make any educational decisions prior to planning the building.

The architectural selection process can take various forms, but most have common elements. First, depending on the size of a district, the planning department, chief engineer, business manager, superintendent, or other designated office should assemble and maintain a list of all registered and licensed architectural firms that have expressed interest in being considered for school district projects. The firms are then asked to complete a standard form and this becomes the list of architects and/or engineers to be considered. The list is reviewed annually at least, and periodically updated to include new firms. The procedures for selecting an architect include the following four steps:

1. The district advertises (by sending a letter to firms on the list) indicating that a job is available.

2. The advertisement outlines the nature of the project and includes a brief outline of the program.

3. Firms wishing to be considered are asked to submit a proposal to the district within a specified time.

4. A committee, internal to the district, reviews the proposals and selects a limited number (probably three or no more than five) to be interviewed. The committee is composed of people representing the district's central administration, the unit (school or building) that is the subject of the project, and a representative of the department responsible for construction. Note that when projects with an estimated cost of more than $500,000 are being planned, the screening committee may have a more comprehensive set of participants.

The committee evaluates the firms expressing interest using the following criteria:

1. Experience in similar building types

2. The qualifications of the firm's principal personnel and proposed consultants

3. Past experience in doing district work

4. Availability to meet the district's timetable

5. Record for completing projects on scheduled dates

6. Availability of competent, adequate staff

7. Amount of work recently done for the district

8. Current workload that may have an impact on the proposed project

9. Past performance in meeting budgets

10. Understanding the project and building type

The committee then ranks the firms for further interviews and evaluation by the committee.

During its final evaluation, the committee considers, in particular, projects that have been designed by each firm, including a review of project costs and the firm's ability to meet budget constraints. The committee ranks the firms and begins negotiations with the top-ranked firm. Following the completion of negotiations, the committee recommends that the board approve a contract with the firm selected.

The AIA has published a new guide for working with architects: *Building Relationships.* The guide is divided into two parts. The first part presents an overview of the design and construction process; the second part consists of worksheets and other materials that take you through the process step by step. The guide is available from your local architect or AIA component or through the AIA in Washington, D.C.

The first step in designing an educational facility is being retained to do the project. A few words of advice about landing the job: The architect who discusses the prospective client's problem generally receives the commission. The architect who spends the interview talking about his or her background and the number of awards won is generally unsuccessful. The following points should be considered before going to the interview:

1. Who will be conducting the interview? What are their backgrounds?

2. What is the real project for which you are being interviewed? Are there any hidden agendas?

3. Where will you be interviewed? Is the room conducive to audiovisual presentations? Will you have time to set up such a presentation? If so, how many slides should be included?

4. Have you visited the site in question? Taking slides or making sketches on the site to use in your presentation is a good idea.

5. Who will be on your team, and who will be at the interview? Everyone brought to an interview should make a contribution, even if brief.

6. Who will field questions? Always leave time for questions and discussion. Be prepared to start things off if no questions come quickly.

7. Will you prepare any kind of material to leave behind? If so, gear it to the client's problem and include a time schedule, a listing of personnel who will be directly involved, and a list of references including letters from former clients, if possible.

At one of the most successful interviews this author attended, the architect took the selection committee on a tour of a school to be remodeled, pointing out deficiencies and suggesting design solutions. No sketches, but verbal comments on things that could be done to update the facility made a strong first impression.

The American Institute of Architects offers a helpful publication, *A Beginner's Guide to Architectural Services,* which explains how the architect (1) solves problems, (2) can save money for the client, and (3) makes the client's life easier. These three points are a basic outline to use in preparing for an interview.

Also note the following suggestions based on one administrator's extensive experience as a client:

• Do not call the school district asking for an interview after the bond issue. Architectural selection generally comes prior to a bond issue.

- Architects should not just quote a fee for doing a job. A better approach is to indicate how much time will be spent. Spell out the tasks and estimate the time that will be devoted to each.

- Know the client. Where is their emphasis? Take time to know the details of the project. More time spent upfront will minimize problems later on.

- Prepare as complete documents as possible. Construction costs generally increase if contractors do not understand the documents.

How to Work with School Boards

The major area of dispute between school building owners and architects is who is in charge of supervision. To avoid misunderstandings, the school building owner should be "gently reminded" that the architect is not a field supervisor. The problem may arise because architects promise something that sounds like field supervision in interviews. So architects should be sure to tell the client up front that the firm is not going to provide field supervision.

Such promises often lead the client toward great expectations that are dashed when the first change order comes in. It is important that the client be made aware that

- Architects cannot detail everything, although they do approve or disapprove all shop drawings.

- Questions are a normal part of the building process.

- Architects cannot control market factors which affect bids.

- Contractors have total control of the building *process.*

- When disputes arise, the architect must remain neutral, taking the side of neither the client nor the contractor.

- The role of the architect is to recommend, and the role of the client is to make decisions.

Everyone has heard stories of projects on which everything that could go wrong did. In one particular case, the school board believed that if the architect had done his job, none of the problems would have occurred. The administrator felt caught in the middle because she understood the role of the architect, but the board did not. The problem was compounded by the fact that the board changed during the project. This led to the recommendation that both the client and the board should document every decision, no matter how small, made during the building process. On the positive side, the administrator pointed out that the district now has a "beautiful, functional building" and she would hire the same architect again. It is important to note, therefore, that the "problem project" is in the minority, but it is generally the one that gets the most publicity. The majority of projects are cooperative successes that come in on time, on budget, and result in proper environments for the delivery of education.

Learning the Community Perspective

It is the rare building program today that does not include input from the community. This generally takes the form of subcommittees addressing specialized areas, such as athletic facilities, site selection, curriculum, and so on. Working with these groups is an excellent time for the architect to learn more about the community's aspirations for education. Surprisingly, these are often not the same as that of the school administration. Being present as a resource at community meetings can help the architect avoid advocating an unpopular concept. For example, at one such meeting the architect discovered that the community for some reason hated pink brick.

CRS Architects under the direction of William Caudill was expert at learning what the community would buy. The firm developed a design process famous for its teams of so-called squatters. Caudill would lead a team of energetic architects, planners, and consultants in setting up shop, usually in the client's board room. Through a series of intense work sessions with the various interest groups, the squatters would help shape a consensus. The process is still in use; some call it a *charrette;* others, a *design-in.* No matter the term, the goal is to get all ideas and concerns out in the open. Commenting on the process, Caudill once said: "Our friends in the profession thought that the squatters process was the worst device that could possibly be. At least two articles were written condemning the system. The chief argument was that to bring clients in would nip good ideas in the bud. And there is some truth to that. That's the chance you take with the squatters. But we think it's worth it."

Today, it is usually the client who insists on some form of architect-community involvement in the planning process. It is no longer a question of *whether* to involve the community. It is a question of *how.*

Gaining the Child's Perspective

When asked to design a school, a group of second-grade students in Atlanta visualized a free-flowing, domelike structure with a soft, resilient surface on the interior. The children reasoned that if a school is supposed to encourage spontaneous activity and freedom in learning, a free-flowing shape would work best. If you ask a child to design or draw a classroom, the result usually includes at least one circle within a traditional rectangular space. Architects seem to draw space-relationship diagrams in circles, but design the actual space in squares. What happens from concept to design? Do we lose the child's perspective?

In a delightful book, one observer commented: "Rooms should not be traps, especially schoolrooms. They need not be. They can enclose, without imprisoning—and if they succeed in this, they usually contain livelier classes, better learners. They are some people who have come out in favor of austere, barracks-like schools—in some cases of actual discomfort. But these people include few children."[2]

One way to gain a child's perspective is to sit in classrooms to see how the space is used, to see if the environment is used easily by the child or if the room is so restrictive that there is little choice but to stay put in the assigned chair. It is not easy to be a child again, but it is rewarding to talk to children—at any age—on what they do or do not like about a school building.

California architect Gaylaird Christopher feels strongly about designing a school from the child's perspective. He asks, "How often have we gone to a board meeting and never heard kids mentioned once." In a preliminary report of a study he is heading on the effect of architecture on education he notes that most successful schools appear to follow through on their most important ideals down to the smallest detail. He also observes that in some schools he visited there is as much as a 20 percent improvement in test scores the first year children were in a new facility.

"Learning itself cannot be poured out like milk; children must be interested. It is the good teacher, who really interests them . . . but a personable building, with the mark of individual aspirations on it, is appropriate to the process, too," concludes Walter McQuade.

Other Important Issues

A number of crucial issues remain for the architect to deal with when designing a school. They range from how equipping a school for today's advanced technology can affect a design, to choosing furniture and equipment and providing for modernization, specialized spaces, and security. Another major concern is how to organize the work into efficient and effective building phases for the successful, on-budget completion of the project.

How Technology Affects School Design

It is the rare school district today that is not concerned about the use of technology in the delivery of education. A major issue is rapid obsolescence: what is planned today may be outmoded tomorrow. The architect is often faced with planning for a program that is certain to change.

The computer lab as we know it today may no longer exist in secondary schools in not too many years. It may well continue at the elementary level where the youngster—younger every year—learns keyboarding and becomes comfortable with the use of technology. Because the computer is moving into the classroom, all classrooms should be designed to have one or more terminals and a television set. It is best to locate the TV receiver on a portable cart because the sets are constantly changing and it does not make sense to go to the expense or trouble to mount them permanently from the ceiling. It does suggest a secured closet in each classroom where equipment can be stored when not in use.

Every space—educational, administrative, and supportive—should be wired for use of technology. What is needed is a telephone jack, electrical outlets, and cable access. The choice of the kind of cable should include copper cable and fiber optic, although fiber optic should be the choice for those equipping for future capacity. State guidelines usually dictate the minimum square footage per computer station. Generally, this is about 35 square feet for a basic work station, with 60 square feet recommended for computers with computer-aided design capability.

In a certain series of catalogs of computer furniture and equipment, the lack of visible wires in the illustrations was noticeable. Everything was neat and orderly. However, there are wires—lots of them—connected to technology. The architect needs to take this into consideration when designing places for work stations. Manufacturers are trying to cope with this problem. Demand has forced them to design computer furniture that understands the wire problem and the fact that users come in varying sizes. While the architect is becoming more aware of the need to address the impact of educational technology on the environment, another main concern often overlooked is lighting. Glare on the terminal or TV screen should be kept to a minimum. Task lighting or indirect lighting should be considered in spaces where computer terminals are to be used. This can be accomplished by lighting under cabinets or reflected off the ceiling.

Technology is here to stay. If one thing is certain, the hardware will get smaller and be more portable. Planning for what is here today can only promote future use.

Furniture and Equipment

Furnishing and equipping schools was once a fairly simple matter. The earliest schools were furnished with benches with a desk for the teacher at the front of the room. Each pupil would respond to the teacher's questions by either standing and reciting or writing the answer on a slate, which was then presented to the teacher for grading or comments. One advantage of this approach was the minimized need for paper and other supplies. Books were scarce, so storage needs were no great concern.

Eventually a work surface was placed in front of the pupil's benches and later the well-known chair-desk combination, usually bolted to the floor, made an appearance. A large chalkboard was mounted on a wall, generally behind the teacher's desk. Today desks are unbolted from the floor, permitting even more freedom of grouping and room arrangements.

Changes in school furniture and equipment have come as a response to program. As schools moved from the one-room schoolhouse to multirooms arranged by age or grade to specialized spaces (libraries, music rooms, art rooms, cafeterias), furniture and equipment was designed to meet new needs. The open-plan school required furniture that moved. Special storage units became "walls." When tight budgets influenced schools to design cafeterias to serve as a multiuse physical education area and/or as an auditorium or assembly space, the response was stackable, folding, or combination tables and seats that could disappear into the walls much like the old Murphy bed.

With technology has come new demands for not only power access but also furniture that can accommodate all the storage needs that go with electronic paraphernalia. Audiovisual equipment advanced from the old-fashioned movie projector to slide and overhead projectors, television, and VCRs. Even the traditional chalkboard is in question when walls you can write on are now available.

Progress is often slow. Teachers are often reluctant to accept a new concept. As one teacher responded when asked her opinion of replacing the chalkboard with overhead projectors to make use of a white wall, "I'm not much for these new-fangled ideas." One planner has called this fear of changes "equipmentphobia."

Changes do occur and will continue to do so. When carpeting was first introduced into schools, children responded by doing projects on the floor. Several years ago on a tour of Irish schools, a stop was made at a school where carpeting had just been installed, the staff required all students to leave their shoes in the entrance vestibule. At an Oklahoma elementary school this sign is over the entrance to a computer room: "Enter quietly with hands behind [your] back."

School furniture and equipment tend to reflect the attitude and education philosophies of the school. An influential school of the 1970s was the Early Learning Center in Stamford, Connecticut. Margaret Skutch, its founder and director, was much in demand as a resource person for staff meetings all over the country. At one such meeting while showing slides of the facility she was questioned about the low storage and activity units of concrete blocks topped by boards painted white. The slides showed children using them as desks, game boards, even standing on them as on a stage. The question: "Don't those boards get dirty with all that activity?" The answer: "I sincerely hope so because then we know we've succeeded." That answer alone told much about the teaching approach and student response at that school. There was no "enter quietly with hands behind backs" here. The environment and the furniture and equipment reflected this accepting approach.

Crow Island School in Winnetka, Illinois, continues to be considered an influential school because over 50 years after it opened its doors the administration, the teachers, the parents, and the pupils still follow and believe in the inspirational planning accomplished by the group that worked with the facility's architect in 1940, which was made up of the same constituents. The original furniture for Crow Island was designed by the Saarinens. Although much of it has been retired from use—and used it was—pieces of the original furniture are on display in the school to remind all of the importance of this aspect of the building. What made this furniture so good was its attention to the needs of children and its respect for their size and activities.

In place of rigid tables and chairs, one school district started experimenting with movable chalkboards with snap-up shelves, large hollow blocks, tote trays with hard-surface writing tops, inflated inner tubes for sitting in, or the addition of brightly painted plywood tops, for sitting at. Stadium seats—the kind taken to football games—and pillows were used for floor seating. A neighboring district found furniture a stumbling block in creating open-plan environments. The educators wanted a basic collection of things to sit on, stand on, and show slides on. A requirement was that those "things" had to be pushable on carpeted floor. Another requirement was that they had to be sufficiently lightweight for elementary school children to move about.

What about tomorrow? The increased use of technology in education will probably have the major impact, requiring furniture that will adjust to the user's size and other needs, such as an understanding that left-handed people are uncomfortable with right-handed furniture.

The manufacturers are obviously trying to meet such needs. Demand has forced them to produce computer furniture just as it has forced the architect to design environments for computer education without really knowing what the environment should be. For the most part, however, educators are not able to define space or furniture needs for computer education. Consequently, the development of furniture and equipment for the mass school market has not kept pace with building design which houses that furniture. And this is probably the key. The space is designed for a specific program, a specific need. The furniture and equipment, if not custom-designed, is not. If ever there was a time when cooperation was needed among educators, architects, and manufacturers, it is now. All parties have too much at stake to make too many mistakes.

Perhaps the situation will always be this way. Really good environments will be custom-styled for the user. One obvious solution is a maximum of built-in furniture and equipment. Schools that have a total learning environment will be respected by generation after generation of user.

Modernization Criteria

The following four concerns should be addressed when considering modernization of a school building:

1. *Safety.* If the building is not safe, or cannot be made safe, it is not a proper place for children.

2. *Education adequacy.* If the building cannot be adapted to meet the educational goals of the district, it should be abandoned.

3. *Location adequacy.* If the building is located in an area where there aren't enough students, or if projections indicate that there will not be enough students within the next few years, it does not make sense to keep the old building.

4. *Site adequacy.* If the site is too small to meet the current standards and there is no way of adding to it, the building should be abandoned unless the district is willing to compromise.

The following rule of thumb is suggested to guide the decision of when to modernize: If it is possible to provide academic programs equivalent to those offered elsewhere in the district in an existing building without expending more than 50 percent of the estimated cost of a new building, modernization becomes a feasible route and a sound investment. This is based on a projected additional life for the building of from 20 to 30 years.

Specialized Spaces

Specialized spaces, either freestanding or as additions to an existing facility, represent a design challenge facing today's architect. Common among this building type is the fieldhouse. These facilities are generally designed for community use. The very nature of their use leads to a clearspan structure that permits indoor running tracks and multicourt sports activities. Natatoriums are another example of a specialized facility being added to schools in all parts of the country. The growing importance of aquatic sports at the university level, coupled with television exposure the sport is receiving, are contributing factors.

The fine-arts center is another building type gaining in popularity. This facility, far more than the traditional school auditorium, is often planned in cooperation with another community funding agency to become a center of community cultural activities. The challenge is to design a facility that can properly house student, community, and professional performances of theater, dance, and music. Many such facilities include a visual-arts complex designed with space for both the creative arts and a public display gallery.

Libraries are no longer just libraries. They are resource, media, or instructural resource centers, or any other designation that is currently in vogue. One thing they all have in common, no matter what they are called, is they are centers for more than a collection of printed materials.

A valuable tip for any architect designing a specialized facility is to add an expert consultant on that specialty to the design team. Specialized spaces requires specialized know-how.

Security: A Necessary Design Factor

Security of school property has become a major concern of school districts. Unfortunately, the problem is not confined to the big cities. Vandalism, theft, arson, and drug abuse continue to be an ever-increasing problem in most school districts. Most school systems of any size now have a director of security, and some even have their own police force. There is even an association of school security directors, and certain commercial organizations specialize in solving security problems for education institutions. Consider the following statistics:

- Vandalism costs schools nationwide more than $1 billion annually.

- Burglaries occur five times more often in schools than in business.

- Between 1982 and 1986, an average of 5500 fires affected elementary and high-school buildings each year, resulting in an average of $56 million in annual direct property damage.

- According to the National Fire Protection Association, most school fires were of suspicious origins.

- Because of their high risk, many school districts are unable to buy insurance because of prohibitive rates.

- While urban schools have suffered from vandalism for years, it is now reaching critical proportions in suburban and rural areas as well. One security firm, Sonitrol, headquartered in Orlando, Florida, has prepared a checklist of security guidelines. Architects should consider the design implications of the following recommendations:

- The building

    Ensure convenient vehicle access for night surveillance and fire or police response.

    Avoid blind spots such as doorways, fences, support buildings, and landscaping.

    Place mechanical or electrical devices, such as meters and transformers, in lockable, recessed vaults or within the building structure.

    Mount flagpoles on roof.

    Limit roof and upper-floor access.

- Playgrounds

    Restrict vehicle access.

    Use fences, walls, or landscaping to separate sports and play areas from school buildings. Place signs above reachable height. Avoid raised metallic or wooden letters.

- Landscaping

    Keep trees at least 10 feet from buildings to prevent window and roof access.

    Limit shrubs to low ground cover, and group plants together. Hedging along walks helps channel pedestrian traffic.

- Exterior lighting

    Place wall-mounted or freestanding lights 12 to 14 feet above the ground. Light standards should be constructed of galvanized steel or concrete.

    Use direct light at the facility if the building is patrolled from the exterior.

    Light the school grounds around the facility if the facility is patrolled from within.

Building security is a second line of protection.

- Doors

    Use as few doors as possible and equip key-controlled doors with contacts for alarm purposes.

    Doors should be constructed of steel, aluminum alloy, or solid-core hardwood. Frames should be constructed of pryproof metal. If they are necessary, glass doors should be fully framed and made of burglar-resistant tempered glass.

    Secure high-risk areas such as computer labs, storerooms, and offices with heavy-duty metal, solid-core hardwood doors.

- Windows

    Windows at the end of the hallway are especially susceptible to damage by items thrown or kicked down the hall.

    Avoid using sliding windows and casement windows.

- Lavatories

    Partitions and doors will be more resistant to vandalism if made of laminated plastic.

    Conceal pipes where possible.

    Use alternatives to plate glass mirrors.

- Visitor control and access

    Designate one entrance for use during school hours.

Major Building Phases

To be competitive, today's architect will offer services far beyond those traditionally associated with the profession. Fast-track scheduling, construction management, graphic design, master planning, interior design, energy conservation, land-use analysis, interior design, and a host of other features are usually offered at additional fees. The standard contract generally lists only the following major phases of the process where the architect is involved:

1. Predesign planning or programming

2. Schematic design

3. Design development

4. Construction document preparation

5. Bidding

6. Construction

The architect then translates these items into a project schedule. These graphic interpolations can be straightforward or contain design elements of their own (Fig. 5.1). No two projects are exactly alike, but the steps in planning a school, in general, with the roles of the architect and client outlined, can be documented.

1. Predesign Planning or Programming. Although each job has its own special requirements, the architect's first step is usually taken with the client. Together they analyze the project requirements and conditions with an awareness of budget restrictions, site, occupancy schedule, and educational specifications. The predesign planning process can be expedited if the architect takes part in the development of the educational specifications. This is especially true if a group process is used for specification development.

2. Schematic Design. This is the generally accepted name for the phase where the architect translates the educational program into a design. As noted above, if the architect is involved in the development of the educational specifications, this becomes a process of refining the ideas. Early involvement is particularly important if extensive community and staff involvement is indicated in the planning process. As the educational specifications are developed by either the in-house or outside facilitator, the architect has the opportunity to hear firsthand the preferences of the users. Narrowing the space options from several (or a combination of several) to one solution is the goal of the schematic design phase.

3. Design Development. At this stage the design is finalized, generalities become specifics. Decisions must be made about room size, space relationships, structural system, mechanical and electrical systems, orientation on site, in fact, everything, including development of a more detailed cost estimate for review and approval by the proper local, state, and federal agencies.

4. Construction Document Preparation. These documents include building specifications for every system, detail, and material of the building. It should be noted that *educational specifications* and *architectural specifications* are often confused. They are two distinct and necessary elements of a successful building project. The architectural specifications guide contractors during construction. The plans (working drawings) and specifications are organized into civil, architectural, structural, heating, ventilation, and air conditioning (HVAC), electrical, plumbing, fire protection, landscape, and interior design. Many architectural firms have all the professional disciplines necessary to prepare these documents on staff; others use outside professional consultants. Either way, this is a most critical stage of the project and one where the owner and the educational planner should stay involved to answer questions, and be prepared to make the many decisions necessary to assure a workable final product built within the realities of the budget. Finally, the plans are approved by the client, and a last update of the earlier cost estimates is made. If the estimates indicate that the project is out of line with the budget, this is the time to make design adjustments.

5. Bidding. This is where qualified contractors, using the construction documents as a basis, estimate how much it will cost to actually build the project. To expedite this process, the architect should maintain records of performance of contractors and material suppliers to ensure a qualified list of bidders on each project. An approved list of bidders should be prepared in cooperation with the client. The architect is responsible for notifying contractors of the bidding date. In most states, the question of how the project is bid and who has the right to bid is established by law. By legally required advertisements, letters to encourage contractors to bid, and other means, construction firms are notified as to the date and times when specifications will be available. After receipt and analysis of bids, the architect recommends contract award to the client.

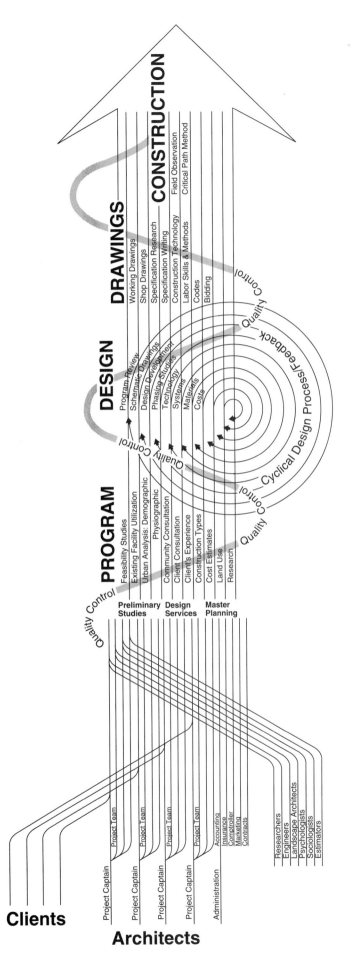

Clients

Architects

PROGRAM

Preliminary Studies
Design Services
Master Planning

Feasibility Studies
Existing Facility Utilization
Urban Analysis: Demographic
Physiographic
Community Consultation
Client Consultation
Client's Experience
Construction Types
Cost Estimates
Land Use
Research

Project Captain
Project Team

Administration
Accounting
Insurance
Comptroller
Marketing
Contracts

Researchers
Engineers
Landscape Architects
Psychologists
Sociologists
Estimators

DESIGN

Program Review
Schematic Drawings
Design Development
Phasing Studies
Technology
Systems
Materials
Costs

Quality Control

Cyclical Design Process/Feedback

DRAWINGS

Working Drawings
Shop Drawings
Specification Research
Specification Writing
Construction Technology
Labor Skills & Methods
Codes
Bidding

CONSTRUCTION

Field Observation
Critical Path Method

Figure 5.1. The programming, design, and construction process. *Source:* Richard Fleischman, architect.

6. Construction. The contract is awarded to the construction firm that comes in with bids within the restrictions of the budget. The architectural firm checks the construction firm's shop drawings in detail while the project is under construction. The construction management phase includes the preparation of supplementary detail drawings, the approval of materials and samples, counseling with the contractor on the proper execution of the work, the keeping of accounts and preparation of change orders, and the approval of payments for completed work. According to the size of the project, either periodic on-site visits are needed or a full-time staff person is assigned by the architect to monitor the construction of the facility. Job reports—on an at least weekly basis—are kept by this representative and then condensed and submitted to the client. Often monthly progress photographs are required from the contractor to further document progress. Reviews of construction progress should be scheduled with the client periodically or by request during the building phase. These review sessions should include representatives from the architectural firm, contractor, and any engineers or consultants whose area is under discussion. Final inspection is made by the architect with the client when the building is completed prior to issuing the final certificate for payment. All bonds, guarantees, and related documents are collected by the architect and delivered to the client.

Working Together

Anyone who has visited many schools built during the last 30 years knows that some of them are poorly planned. Still, a significant number of good buildings are a tribute to all involved in their planning. Successful schools tend to have seven things in common:

1. The schools did not just happen. They resulted from a definitely stated program. The community stated what they wanted and why. The architect did not operate in a vacuum. The architect was truly able to approach design using the simple, but often ignored, principle that form follows function. Professionals bring experience to the table. Both the client and the architect have definite views of what works. When one particular superintendent was questioned on why he thought a project was so successful, he answered that neither he nor his architect would accept anything that was not agreed on by both. Of course, there was give and take, and all decisions were based on a reasonable and defensible rationale. Neither party—client nor architect—should accept anything he or she does not like.

2. Those involved in the planning were not afraid to say, "I don't know." Problems occur when one person plays the role of the all-knowing expert. The planning of the New Orleans Center for the Creative Arts is a good example. This author served as the educational consultant but regarded this role as more of a facilitator. The staff of professional and (some) well-known actors, musicians, dancers, artists, and writers brought expertise to the process. The result was a real give and take. We learned, for example, that with proper planning space for the various areas of creative art could be shared. As questions were asked, we all agreed that if we really did not know the answer, we would say so. The result, we anticipated, will be a facility that will serve all the arts in an appropriate environment.

3. Charrettes are fine, but they should be the exception, not the rule. Good schools are the result of planning teams that take time to explore, think, and change their minds, realizing that the resulting building will probably be around to serve several generations. A field trip to visit other schools is a wise investment. They should be visited only when they are in operation. Otherwise, the building may look great, but not function properly. When you want to find out about a school, address questions to the teachers, the staff, custodians, and the kids for whom it was supposedly planned in the first place. A good idea is to take a look at a sketch of a classroom designed by a child.

4. Involving the community in the planning process takes time and effort, but the results are worth it. After all, they are going to pay for it, so why should they not have a say? Look back at the Crow Island School. Larry Perkins says the secret of its success can be traced to the input of all parties—including parents in the planning process. Today, parents are not the only ones who should be involved. Chances are that people without children in the schools outnumber those with children. Get them involved and consider their ideas and needs and you gain valuable support for the project. When you have lots of people involved in the process, you must keep your cool. At a public meeting where this author presented the educational programs for a new 2500-student high school, one woman in the audience objected to the fact that there were three cots for girls and only two for boys in the health suite. The author asked her "Do you want me to take one away from the girls or add one for the boys?"

5. Let the dust settle before you start listening to complaints on what is wrong with the school. Remember that most of the occupants are moving from a familiar environment to a new, strange one. It is a good idea to have a "how to use" training session with all who will use the facility. Technology is a good example. If no one explains how to use the new electronics school, it may be ignored or even berated. Do not forget the custodial staff. The mechanical and electrical system may be foreign to them, and an in-service training session will pay big dividends.

6. After the building has been in operation for at least one semester, conduct a postoccupancy evaluation. Mistakes were probably made or some things simply do not work as designed. Find out and make all possible corrections. Then do not make the same mistake on the next project.

7. Make sure the school stays in good condition. Neglect of an expensive investment is a sin. Maintain it, and repair things that break. A preventive-maintenance program is the best investment a school district can make. If this had occurred, we would not be hearing all the horror stories about the big-city schools.

Good advice to architects was expressed by Lawrence Lord, a principal of Lord, Aeck & Sargent in Atlanta, "It takes a lot of time to get to know the school board client; every jurisdiction has its own set of priorities and needs, and we are obliged to wear different hats for each school board. This is not easy, and the first project you take with a particular jurisdiction is not likely to be as profitable as other project types."

As all involved in the process know, building schools can be one of the most rewarding careers. Perhaps the most gratifying feedback comes from the schools' users themselves. One story tells it best. Several years ago architect Samuel Caudill was touring Aspen High School, which he had designed not long before. As Caudill walked down the corridor, one youngster turned to his friend and said with a note of pride, "That's our architect." That may have been one of the happiest days in Caudill's life—a fitting tribute to every architect of educational facilities.

Notes

1. Educational Facilities Laboratories, *The Cost of a Schoolhouse,* EFL, 1960, p. 138.

2. Walter McQuade, *Schoolhouse,* Simon & Schuster, New York, 1958.

Coming Full Circle

In Chap. 2 we talked about the one-room schoolhouse of yesterday. It seems only appropriate to end with two recent examples of one-teacher schools. Both were designed by the Seattle firm of Larsen Lagerquist Morris, Architects (now Largerquist & Morris).

Stuart Island School
Stuart Island, Washington

Larsen Lagerquist Morris, architect

1000 square feet

10 to 20 students

Northernmost of the American San Juans, a group of islands off the coast of Washington, Stuart Island has no ferry service, power lines, or telephones, and the children of the 60 year-round adult residents walk to school along forest paths. When the total population of young scholars swelled to 12 in the late 1980s, it became clear that the existing public school, a white clapboard structure built in 1901, was no longer adequate. Residents petitioned successfully for state funds to erect a 1000-square-foot classroom facility but balked when the regional school district proposed shipping in trailer modules for the purpose. The fan-shaped plan that was eventually built lends itself to alternate use as classroom, theater, or meeting hall, while maximizing solar gain through south-facing windows and a double clerestory. This daylighting won special praise from Stuart Islanders, who consider the noise of power generation a public nuisance.

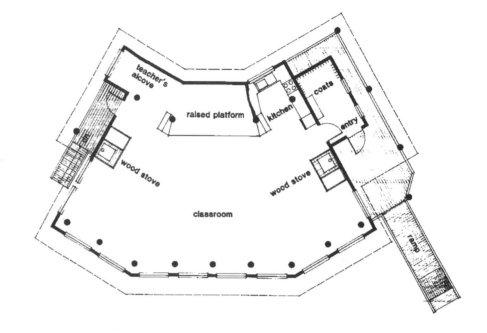

South facade.

View of interior.

Myers Chuck School
Myers Chuck, Alaska

Larsen Lagerquist Morris, architect

2400 square feet

10 to 20 students

Making the most of resources at hand is one of the earliest lessons anyone learns in Myers Chuck, Alaska. Founded in 1880s, this isolated fishing village at the tip of the Cleveland Peninsula has neither roads nor utilities and is accessible only by boat or float-plane. The 2400-square-foot frame structure replaces the one-room rented shack where local children used to learn the three Rs (reading, writing, and arithmetic).

Flexible enough to serve the academic and recreational needs of kindergarten through grade 12 and to double as a community center for Myers Chuck residents of all ages, the project also includes living quarters for one permanent teacher and temporary accommodations for instructors, nurses, performing artists, and other visitors who fly in on a circuit through the regional school district.

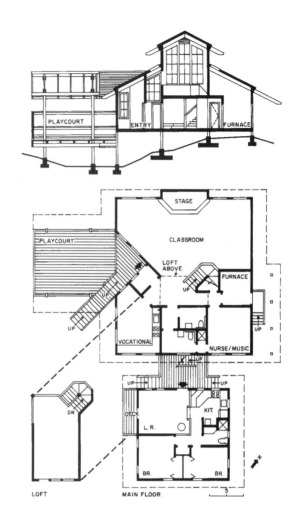

The interior is flexible enough to accommodate both small and large groups.

The school sits comfortably on its wooded site.

6

Where to Get Help

Educational Facilities Laboratories (EFL) was established in 1958 by the Ford Foundation to guide and encourage constructive change in education and other "people serving" institutions. In this role, EFL served as a clearinghouse for information on school facility planning. In 1971 the Ford Foundation began phasing out its general support of EFL, and EFL made the successful transition to being a self-supporting organization. In 1979 EFL became an operating division of the Academy for Educational Development. When no group emerged to fill the information clearinghouse role, EFL personnel, by default, continued to field questions from those seeking school planning help. In 1990 when this author retired as head of the EFL division, this effectively signaled the end of EFL. But to this day, calls come to his office from all parts of the country from new groups of people seeking information and ideas as they face the challenge of planning educational environments. Unfortunately, there is no school facilities division at the federal level, and no one organization has emerged to fill the void left by EFL's disappearance. There are, however, sources of information that can be tapped into as a beginning point in the planning process.

Sources

Association Conferences and Conventions

Excellent sources of information are the annual national and regional conferences of several organizations. The ones listed below have architectural exhibitions of educational projects as well as programs and seminars devoted to related subjects. In addition, they often have publications available on school planning issues.

American Association of School
   Administrators
1801 North Moore Street
Arlington, Virginia 22209-9988
(703) 875-0753

Association of School Business
   Officials/International
11401 North Shore Drive
Reston, Virginia 22090-4232
(703) 478-0405

National School Boards Association
1680 Duke Street
Alexandria, Virginia 22314-3407
(703) 838-6722

The three organizations listed above have state associations with state
conventions.

Council of Educational Facility
   Planners/International
941 Chatham Lane, Suite 217
Columbus, Ohio 43221
(614) 442-1811

International Society for Educational
   Planning
c/o Educational Administration
Purdue University
G-10 South Campus Courts
West Lafayette, Indiana 47907

Magazines and Periodicals

The architectural and educational magazines often devote entire issues to
presentations of educational buildings.

Architectural

Architectural Record
1221 Avenue of the Americas
New York, New York 10020

Architecture
1130 Connecticut Avenue, N.W.,
   Suite 625
Washington, D.C. 20036

Progressive Architecture
P.O. Box 1361
Stamford, Connecticut 06904

Educational

*American School & University
   Magazine*
401 North Broad Street
Philadelphia, Pennsylvania 19108

School Product News
1111 Chester Avenue
Cleveland, Ohio 44114

The School Administrator
1801 North Moore Street
Arlington, Virginia 22209

Government Agencies

State Departments of Education. The quality of information about
facilities coming from state Departments of Education is not consistent.
However, some states, such as California, North Carolina, Florida, and
New Jersey to name just a few, often have excellent planning and design
documents. The following is a complete list of state education agency
addresses:

Alabama Department of Education
501 Dexter Avenue
481 State Office Building
Montgomery, Alabama 36130

Alaska State Department of
  Education
Goldbelt Place
P.O. Box F
Juneau, Alaska 99811-0500

Arizona Department of Education
1535 West Jefferson
Phoenix, Arizona 85007

Arkansas Department of Education
4 State Capitol Mall
Little Rock, Arkansas 72201

California Department of Education
721 Capitol Mall
P.O. Box 944272
Sacramento, California 94244-2720

Colorado Department of Education
201 East Colfax Avenue
Denver, Colorado 80203-1705

Connecticut Department of Education
165 Capitol Avenue
P.O. Box 2219
Hartford, Connecticut 06106

Delaware Department of Public
  Instruction
Post Office 1402
Dover, Delaware 19903

District of Columbia Public Schools
415 Twelfth Street N.W.
Washington, D.C. 20004

Florida Department of Education
Capitol Building, Room PL 116
Tallahassee, Florida 32399

Georgia Department of Education
2066 Twin Towers East
Atlanta, Georgia 30334-5020

Hawaii Department of Education
Post Office Box 2360
Honolulu, Hawaii 96804

Idaho Department of Education
650 West State Street
Boise, Idaho 83720

Illinois State Board of Education
100 North First Street
Springfield, Illinois 62777-0001

Indiana Department of Education
State House, Room 229
Indianapolis, Indiana 46204-2798

Iowa Department of Education
Grimes State Office Building
East 14th and Grand Streets
Des Moines, Iowa 50319-0146

Kansas Department of Education
120 East Tenth Street
Topeka, Kansas 66612

Kentucky Department of Education
1725 Capitol Plaza Tower
Frankfort, Kentucky 40601

Louisiana Department of Education
Post Office Box 94064
Baton Rouge, Louisiana 70804-9064

Maine Department of Educational
  and Cultural Services
State House, Station No. 23
Augusta, Maine 04333

Maryland Department of Education
200 West Baltimore Street
Baltimore, Maryland 21201

Massachusetts Department of
  Education
Quincy Center Plaza
1385 Hancock Street
Quincy, Massachusetts 02169

Michigan Department of Education
P.O. Box 30008
Lansing, Michigan 48909

Minnesota Department of Education
712 Capitol Square Building
550 Cedar Street
St. Paul, Minnesota 55101

Mississippi State Department of
  Education
Post Office Box 771, High Street
Jackson, Mississippi 39205-0771

Missouri Department of Elementary
  and Secondary Education
Post Office Box 480
Jefferson City, Missouri 65102

Montana Office of Public Instruction
State Capitol
Helena, Montana 59620

Nebraska Department of Education
301 Centennial Mall South
Post Office Box 94987
Lincoln, Nebraska 68509

Nevada State Department of
    Education
400 West King Street
Capitol Complex
Carson City, Nevada 89710

New Hampshire Department of
    Education
101 Pleasant Street
State Office Park South
Concord, New Hampshire 03301

New Jersey Department of Education
225 West State Street, CN 500
Trenton, New Jersey 08625

New Mexico State Department of
    Education
Education Building
300 Don Gaspar
Santa Fe, New Mexico 87501-6516

New York State Education
    Department
111 Education Building
Albany, New York 12234

North Carolina Department of Public
    Instruction
Education Building
116 West Edenton Street
Raleigh, North Carolina 27603-1712

North Dakota State Department of
    Public Instruction
State Capitol
600 Boulevard Avenue East
Bismarck, North Dakota 58505-0164

Ohio Department of Education
65 South Front Street, Room 808
Columbus, Ohio 43266-0308

Oklahoma Department of Education
Oliver Hodge Memorial Education
    Instruction Building
2500 North Lincoln Blvd.
Oklahoma City, Oklahoma 73105-4599

Oregon Department of Education
700 Pringle Parkway SE
Salem, Oregon 97310

Pennsylvania Department of
    Education
P.O. Box 911
333 Market Street
Harrisburg, Pennsylvania 17126-
    0333

Rhode Island Department of
    Education
22 Hayes Street
Providence, Rhode Island 02908

South Carolina State Department of
    Education
1006 Rutledge Building
1429 Senate Street
Columbia, South Carolina 29201

South Dakota Department of
    Education and Cultural Affairs
Division of Elementary/Secondary
    Education
Pierre, South Dakota 57501

Tennessee State Department of
    Education
100 Cordell Hull Building
Nashville, Tennessee 37219

Texas Education Agency
William B. Travis Building
1701 North Congress Avenue
Austin, Texas 78701

Utah State Office of Education
250 East 500 South
Salt Lake City, Utah 84111

Vermont Department of Education
120 State Street
Montpelier, Vermont 05602-2703

Virginia Department of Education
Post Office Box 6Q
Fourteenth and Franklin Streets
Richmond, Virginia 23216-2060

Washington State Department of
    Public Instruction
Old Capitol Building
Mail Stop FG-11
Olympia, Washington 98504

West Virginia State Department of
Education
Capitol Complex
Building B, Room 358
Charleston, West Virginia 25305

Wisconsin Department of Public
Instruction
P.O. Box 7841
125 South Webster Street
Madison, Wisconsin 53707

Wyoming Department of Education
Hathaway Building
Cheyenne, Wyoming 82002

American Samoa Department of
Education
Pago-Pago, Tutuila
American Samoa 96799

Guam Department of Education
P.O. Box DE
Agana, Guam 96910

Commonwealth of the Northern
Mariana Islands
Board of Education
P.O. Box 1370 CK
Saipan, MP 96950

Commonwealth of Puerto Rico
Department of Education
P.O. Box 759
Hato Rey, Puerto Rico 00919

Virgin Islands Department of
Education
44–46 Kongens Gade
Charlotte Amalie
St. Thomas, Virgin Islands 00802

The American Institute of Architects. The AIA has an active Committee on Architecture for Education whose materials are available through the national, state, or local offices. This group researches and publishes working papers on a variety of subjects ranging from asbestos removal to facilities for day-care centers. The committee keeps updated a slide (soon to be video) presentation on school facility design. Committee meetings (four per year) are scheduled in different parts of the country and are open to interested parties.

American Institute of Architects
1735 New York Avenue N.W.
Washington, D.C. 20006
(202) 626-7300

Contact: Liaison, Committee on
Architecture for Education

Special Resources. Practically every aspect of education has its own association. A few are listed here. A good specialized resource is the person in your school district responsible for that area. Chances are they belong to the corresponding association.

American Association for Adult and
Continuing Education
1112 16th Street N.W., Suite 420
Washington, D.C. 20036
(202) 463-6333

American Association for Community
and Junior Colleges
One Dupont Circle, Suite 510
Washington, D.C. 20036-1110
(202) 728-0200

American Library Association
50 East Huron Street
Chicago, Illinois 60611
(312) 944-6780

Association for Childhood Education
International
11141 Georgia Avenue, Suite 200
Wheaton, Maryland 20902-4637
(301) 942-2443

National Association of Elementary
  School Principals
1615 Duke Street
Alexandria, Virginia 22314-3406
(703) 684-3345

National Association of Secondary
  School Principals
1904 Association Drive
Reston, Virginia 22091-1502
(703) 860-0200

National Association of Independent
  Schools
11 Dupont Circle N.W., Suite 210
Washington, D.C. 20036-1303
(202) 265-3500

National Trust for Historic
  Preservation
1785 Massachusetts Avenue N.W.
Washington, D.C. 20036-2117
(202) 673-4000

American School Food Service
  Association
1600 Duke Street, 7th Floor
Alexandria, Virginia 22314
(703) 739-3900

American Vocational Association
1410 King Street
Alexandria, Virginia 22314-2715

Energy. The increased interest in energy conservation has resulted in
more activity from agencies at the state level. A good source of information
is through your state's office of energy management or energy information
center. Many states are currently conducting workshops for school planners.
Your local utility companies will have publications available to help you
plan an energy savings program.

Early Childhood. On the twenty-fifth anniversary of the Head Start program, the University of New Mexico School of Architecture received a federal grant from Head Start to develop and test a demonstration classroom
for early-childhood education and care. For more information about the
"Head Start Classroom of the Future," contact

Dr. Anne Taylor
University of New Mexico
School of Architecture
2414 Central, S.E.
Albuquerque, New Mexico 87131

Conclusion

The material presented in this book is based on this author's work, observations, column in *American School and University* magazine, and other writings. Much material, especially historic, borrows freely from the extensive library of Educational Facilities Laboratories. Other sources include many professional contacts with past and present members of the American Institute of Architects' Committee on Architecture for Education.

An attempt has been made to give credit where credit is due for other sources. If credit is missing, please accept the author's apologies.

Projects

Chapter 3

Penn High School (1989), p. 91
Osceola, Indiana
Architect: Greiner, Inc. (formerly Daverman) and HMFH, Inc., associated
    architects

Capital High School (1989), p. 93
Santa Fe, N.M.
Architect: Perkins & Will with Mimbres, Inc.

Deerwood Elementary School (1989), p. 96
Egan, Minn.
Architect: Hammel Green and Abrahamson, Inc.

Berkley Community School, addition and renovation (1989), p. 98
Berkley, Mass.
Architect: Earl R. Flansburgh & Associates

Symmes Elementary School (1989), p. 101
Cincinnati, Ohio
Architect: Baxter Hodell Donnelly Preston, Inc.

P.S. 234 (1989), p. 103
New York City
Architect: Richard Dattner

Jane S. Roberts Elementary School (1990), p. 106
Dade County, Fla.
Architect: Hervin Romney

Methuen Comprehensive Grammar School (1990), p. 109
Methuen, Mass.
Architect: HMFH Architects

Buckeye Local High School (1990), p. 111
Connorville, Ohio
Architect: Lesko Assocs

B.D. Billinghurst Middle School (1990), p. 113
Reno, Nev.
Architect: Lundahl & Associates

Hope Elementary School (1990), p. 115
Hope, Indiana
Architect: Taft Architects

Oak Ridge and Forestdale K-8 Schools (1990), p. 118
Sandwich, Mass.
Architect: HMFH Architects

Science Magnet School No. 59 (1990), p. 120
Buffalo, N.Y.
Architect: Stieglitz Stieglitz Tries

Warsaw Community High School (1990), p. 122
Warsaw, Indiana
Architect: The Odle, McGuire & Shook Corp. and Perkins & Will

Hunt Elementary School (1990), p. 126
Puyallup, Wash.
Architect: Burr Lawrence Rising & Bates Architects

Forest Bluff School (1990), p. 128
Lake Forest, Ill.
Architect: Booth/Hansen & Associates

Minischools (1990), p. 130
New York City
Architect: Weintraub & di Domenico

Canterbury Elementary School (1990), p. 132
Canterbury, Conn.
Architect: Kaestle Boos Associates, Inc.

Westridge Elementary School (1990), p. 134
West Des Moines, Iowa
Architect: RDG Bussard Dikis, Inc.

Child Care Laboratory (1990), p. 136
Wake Technical Community College,
Raleigh, N.C.
Architect: Haskins, Rice, Savage & Pearce

Oak Brook Elementary School (1991), p. 138
St. Louis, Mo.
Architect: Pearce Turner Nikolajevich

P.S. 233 (1991), p. 140
Queens, New York
Architect: Gran Sultan Associates

Worthington Kilbourne High School (1991), p. 142
Worthington, Ohio
Architect: NBBJ

Mt. Carmel Elementary School (1991), p. 145
Douglas County, Georgia
Architect: Lord Aeck & Sargent

Employee Day Care Center, Ingalls Memorial Hospital (1991), p. 148
Harvey, Ill.
Architect: O'Donnell Wicklund Pigozzi and Peterson Architects, Inc.

University High School (1991), p. 150
Orlando, Fla.
Architect: W.R. Frizzell Architects, Inc.

Chapter 4

Chapter 5

Photographers

Introduction

Chapter 1

Chapter 2

Chapter 3

Charles Haskell Elementary School: Larry J. Keller and James Howard
Stow-Munroe Falls High School: Eric Hanson
Desert View Elementary School: Robert Reck
Gatzert Elementary School: David Melody
Sunderland Elementary School: Nick Wheeler
Penn High School: David Emery and Beth Singer
Capital High School: Gregory Murphey
Deerwood Elementary School: Shin Koyama
Berkley Community School: Nick Wheeler
Symmes Elementary School: Ames Cook
P.S. 234: Norman McGrath and Jeff Goldberg/Esto
Jane S. Roberts Elementary School: Dan Forer
Methuen Comprehensive Grammar School: Steve Rosenthal
Buckeye Local High School: Art Cross
B.D. Billinghurst Middle School: Suzanne Lundahl
Hope Elementary School: Paul Warchol
Oak Ridge and Forestdale K-8 Schools: Steve Rosenthal and Wayne Soverns
Science Magnet School No. 59: K.C. Kratt
Warsaw Community High School: Gregory Murphey
Hunt Elementary School: Kit Burns
Forest Bluff School: Timothy Hursley
Minischools: Weintraub & di Domenico
Canterbury Elementary School: Robert Benson
Westridge Elementary School: King Au
Child Care Laboratory, Wake Technical Community College: Allen Weiss-Weisstudio
Oak Brook Elementary School: Robert Pettus
P.S. 233: David Anderson
Worthington Kilbourne High School: Steven Elbert/LUMEN
Mt. Carmel Elementary School: Jonathan Hillier
Employee Day Care Center, Ingalls Memorial Hospital: Hedrich-Blessing
University High School: W.R. Frizzell Architects
Stuyvesant High School: Cooper, Robertson & Partners and Gruzen Samton Steinglass

Chapter 4

Prototype Elementary School: Gruzen Samton Steinglass
Prototype Elementary School: W. Randolph Schaeffer
Prototype Elementary School: Dan Cornish
Prototype Intermediate School: Richard Dattner
Jean Parker Elementary School: Reid & Tarics
Santa Ana High School: Reid & Tarics
Perry Community Education Complex: Hedrich-Blessing

Chapter 5

Stuart Island School: Gary Vannest
Myers Chuck School: Gary Vannest

Index